MICROPROCESSORS FOR MANAGERS

A Decision-Maker's Guide

Ronald L. Krutz

CBI

CBI PUBLISHING COMPANY, INC.

286 Congress Street

Boston, Massachusetts 02210

*To the three most important people
in my life: Hilda, Sheri, and Lisa.*

Production Editor / Kathy Savago
Text Designer / Karen Mason
Compositor / Modern Graphics, Inc.
Jacket Designer / Jack Schwartz

Library of Congress Cataloging in Publication Data

Krutz, Ronald L., 1938–
  Microprocessors for managers.

  Bibliography: p.
  Includes index.
  1. Microprocessors. 2. Microcomputers. 3. Program-
ming languages (Electronic computers) I. Title.
QA76.5.K773 1983   001.64   82–20700
ISBN 0–8436–1610–5

Printed in the United States of America

Printing (last digit): 9 8 7 6 5 4 3 2 1

CONTENTS

Preface   v

Chapter One   *HISTORY AND PERSPECTIVE*   1

   1.1 • History of the Digital Computer   3

   1.2 • Evolution of the Microprocessor   10

   1.3 • Economic Impact of the
         Microprocessor   15

   1.4 • Trends and Future Considerations   18

Chapter Two   *FUNDAMENTAL DIGITAL BUILDING
               BLOCKS*   21

   2.1 • Background   21

   2.2 • Binary State Representations   21

   2.3 • Logic and Arithmetic Functions   26

   2.4 • Storage and Counting Elements   32

   2.5 • Microprocessor Implementation Utilizing
         Fundamental Building Blocks   38

Chapter Three   *STORAGE MEDIA*   43

   3.1 • Introduction to Semiconductor
         Technology   43

3.2 • Semiconductor Memories   47

3.3 • Disk Storage for Microprocessors   58

3.4 • Comparison of Memory Alternatives   60

Chapter Four   MICROPROCESSORS/MICROCOMPUTERS   63

4.1 • Microprocessor Architectural
Considerations   63

4.2 • Architectural Examples   64

4.3 • Microcomputer Systems   74

4.4 • Interfacing Considerations and
Standards   78

Chapter Five   MICROCOMPUTER SOFTWARE   83

5.1 • Definitions   83

5.2 • Software Design Methodology   87

5.3 • Familiarization With High-level
Languages   92

5.4 • Considerations in Software Development,
Reliability, and Maintenance   100

Chapter Six   ECONOMICS/EVALUATION TECHNIQUES
AND CRITERIA   109

6.1 • Microcomputer Selection Criteria   109

6.2 • Random Logic Versus Microcomputer
Characteristics and Tradeoffs   112

6.3 • Software Considerations   114

Appendix A   ASCII Character Set   119

Appendix B   Microprocessor Applications and Required
Capabilities   121

Glossary   123

Index   133

PREFACE

This text is written for the manager or executive who is in some way involved with microprocessors. The manager may be involved directly, as is an engineering supervisor, or indirectly, as is a vice-president or chief executive officer of a company. In these and similar capacities, the manager must be able to make or influence intelligent decisions about the technical directions, possible problems, expenditures, marketing, software support, maintenance, and potential pitfalls associated with microprocessors and related devices. This book provides the information needed to aid the decision-making process.

Chapter 1 provides a historical overview of the computer industry that concludes with the emergence of the microprocessor. The fact that a single semiconductor company can now produce 50,000 microprocessors each month—when up to this time, the world's total inventory of other types of processors totaled approximately 200,000 units—emphasizes the impact of this "processor-on-a-chip." In this context, technical trends and economic considerations for microprocessor-based products are presented to provide a basis for planning and reviewing future commitment decisions.

Based on the perspective of Chapter 1, the functional fundamentals and vocabulary of digital systems are developed in Chapter 2. Digital basics are covered so that the reader can understand the terminology and functional characteristics of digital building blocks without requiring a detailed study of digital system design and the circuits that make up these building blocks. By studying a typical microprocessor implementation, the reader will see that the microprocessor is nothing more than a combination of these building blocks. An emphasis is placed on the fact that microprocessor hardware designs vary primarily in the number and types of building blocks each has and the way in which these are interconnected. The goal is to enable the reader to understand "generic" microprocessor architecture so that he or she can readily comprehend new devices that will be introduced in the future.

One of the most important portions of a microcomputer hardware system is the means of data and program storage. In Chapter 3, the most pervasive storage methods for microprocessors are introduced and explained. Since semiconductor memories are the dominant means of storage used in microcomputer systems, a brief introduction to semiconductor fabrication technology is provided. Short descriptions of the most popular fabrication technologies are presented in a way that relates the technology to microprocessor and memory characteristics such as cost, speed, and power consumption. Definitions and explanations of the different types of semiconductor memories are provided, including Charged Coupled Device (CCD) and magnetic bubble memories. Disk storage as utilized in microcomputer systems is presented, and the chapter concludes with a tabular summary of the memory alternatives.

Chapter 4 develops the architectural concepts of microprocessors and considerations in performing input and output operations. Specifically, system, hardware, and instruction set architectures are defined; and examples utilizing such microprocessors as the MOS technology 6502, Intel 432 micromainframe, Motorola 68000, and the Zilog Z8000 are presented. Means of handling real-time, priority events are also discussed. The role of microprocessors in utilizing high-level programming languages, such as the new Department of Defense Language, Ada, is presented in light of the emphasis of this topic on the design of the next generation of microprocessors. The chapter concludes with discussions of techniques and devices for coupling the microprocessor to the outside world for the purpose of doing useful work. Microcomputer system development philosophies are also covered and recommendations for a software development "workbench" are given.

By far the most expensive and critical component of the total microcomputer system implementation is software. The specification, development, documentation, testing, and maintenance of software can make the difference between the economic success or failure of a microcomputer project. In order to provide the manager with the background to effectively deal with microcomputer software, Chapter 5 incorporates useful definitions and a software design methodology that together are aimed at imparting principles of structure and accepted good practice. From this general overview of software and development principles, the specifics of programming are introduced. Assembly language is the first type of language discussed, since it provides a bridge from the hardware to the high-level languages utilized with microcomputers. Typical assembly language statements are introduced, followed by examples of their use. The transition is then made to high-level language programming along with discussions of other types of useful support programs. The important concept of structured design of software is then presented along with specific examples. To familiarize the reader with the programming languages BASIC, FORTRAN, Pascal, and Ada, summary descriptions are presented. The features, examples, advantages, and disadvantages of each language relative to typical applications are covered. The chapter concludes with discussions of software development practicalities and the concepts of software reliability and maintainability.

Chapter 6 serves as a unifying medium for the concepts and descriptions of the preceding chapters in the text. This chapter attempts to quantify, to the extent possible, the economics of microprocessor utilization and application. In addition, evaluation techniques for the comparison of microprocessors and associated high-level assembly language tradeoffs are developed. Microcomputer selection criteria are established, including comparisons with a non-microcomputer, random logic approach. The chapter concludes with a discussion of the relationship between system cost and performance and language types and levels, to reemphasize the economic factors associated with microcomputer system implementation.

Chapter One

HISTORY AND PERSPECTIVE

The evolution of the microprocessor has initiated irreversible changes affecting markets, corporate viabilities, productivity patterns, working and recreational habits, and even warfare and social order. This device, which is the culmination of the solid state physics and computational research begun in the 1920's (and earlier if one traces supporting and related efforts), has made once costly and unwieldy digital computational power available at the price of a fast-food hamburger and usable by a six-year-old child.

In order to understand the present and future of the microprocessor, it is important to know its past. As with many other technological developments, its history can be graphically perceived as an expanding tree structure with roots in many areas of science and engineering.

Before proceeding to explore the wealth of contributors to the microprocessor, definitions of this device and its related components are in order. A *processor,* in its general form, comprises an arithmetic logic unit (ALU) and associated storage and control circuitry. The ALU performs arithmetic and logic operations such as the shifting of numbers, ANDing between two binary numbers, ORing between two binary numbers, adding and subtracting of two numbers, and, in some cases, multiplication and division. The associated storage consists of a relatively small number of temporary storage locations for intermediate results, and the control circuitry implements decoding and execution of instructions to the processor. In the 1950's, a processor usually occupied the space of a small room. Now, a processor can be integrated onto a silicon chip approximately 0.2 inches square and is defined as a *micro-processor*.

In order for the microprocessor to function, it requires some supporting chips. The basic requirements are memory for program storage, memory for data storage, input/output circuits, and timing (clock) circuits. These chips combined with the microprocessor form a *microcomputer*. The relationship of the microprocessor and the microcomputer is shown in Figure 1.1.

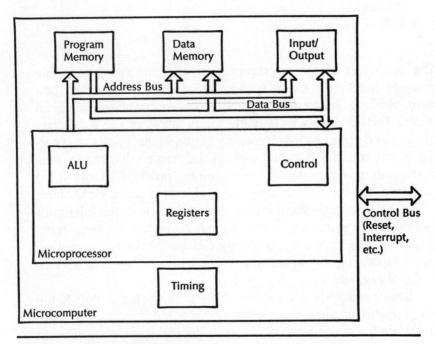

Figure 1.1 The Relationship Between the Microprocessor and Microcomputer

The groups of wires, *buses,* that interconnect the microcomputer are the *address bus* (addresses out of the microprocessor), *data bus* (data in and out of the microprocessor), and the *control bus* (control lines in and out of the microprocessor).

The microprocessor as we know it today is the product of ideas and concepts that were crystallized in the 1920's, nurtured through the 1930's, pressed into military service in the 1940's, emerged as commercial products in the 1950's, and were scaled down to microscopic size in the 1960's and 1970's. A principal product of these developments was the digital computer. The history of the digital computer is an example of the natural evolution of computer and semiconductor technology.

1.1 • HISTORY OF THE DIGITAL COMPUTER

It is difficult to pick the starting point in the history of the digital computer since numerous developments over a few centuries contributed to its emergence. A good starting point may be 1929, when Columbia University established the Columbia University Statistical Bureau under the sponsorship of Thomas J. Watson, chief executive of IBM. IBM supplied this bureau with some of its products, including the mechanical tabulating machine. In 1931, the bureau completed work on a mechanical digital calculator that was based on the designs proposed in the nineteenth century by Charles Babbage, an English mathematician. Watson's continued interest and support of the Columbia University Statistical Bureau led to the establishment of the Thomas J. Watson Astronomical Computing Bureau at Columbia in 1937. A force behind the creation of this bureau was Columbia faculty member Wallace J. Eckert.

Also in 1937, Claude E. Shannon showed in his Master's thesis at M.I.T. that Boolean algebra could be used to design and minimize logic circuits and, vice versa, that logic circuits could implement Boolean functions and addition. Relay circuits were used to implement logic at this time and from 1937 through 1939, the Bell Laboratories Model 1 relay computer was constructed and was the first to use Binary Coded Decimal number representation. A principal in the Model 1 development at Bell Labs was mathematician George R. Stibitz.

The latter years of the 1930's and the early years of the 1940's saw an increase in the development of computing capability. Some of the impetus was provided by the need to rapidly calculate ballistic trajectories. IBM undertook development of another electromechanical calculator based on an idea of a Harvard University graduate student, Howard Aiken. This idea attracted the attention of Wallace Eckert and IBM, and its subsequent development was sponsored by the financial and manpower support of IBM. The result of this effort in 1944 was the first automatic general purpose digital calculator, known as the Automatic Sequence Controlled Calculator or the Harvard Mark I. The Mark I could handle 23 decimal-digit numbers, multiply two of these numbers in three seconds, and add two numbers in 0.3 seconds.

1.1.1 • Development of Vacuum-Tube Computers

A significant contribution to digital computer development began at the University of Pennsylvania Moore School of Electrical Engineering in June, 1943. The Army Ballistic Laboratory provided funding for the development of an idea by Professor John W. Mauchley and graduate student J. Presper Eckert to use vacuum tubes for implementing computing functions. This work resulted in the Electronic Numerical Integrator and Computer, Eniac, in 1946. This vacuum tube computer was comprised of 18,000 vacuum tubes and required 150 kilowatts of power. Eniac could operate on 10-digit numbers in decimal format, multiply two numbers in 2.8 milliseconds (2.8 thousandths of a second), and add two numbers in 0.2 milliseconds. These rates were two to three times faster than rates produced by relay machines of the time.

Eniac had to be programmed by means of patchboard wiring, which was slow and awkward. Storing instructions in memory, as data were stored, and executing these instructions from memory is a technique now commonly used in almost all digital computers. However, this was an innovation when proposed in 1946 for the second version of Eniac, the Edvac (Electronic Discrete Variable Computer).

At about the same time that Eckert and Mauchley were beginning the development of Eniac, the British government's intelligence installation at Bletchley Park was using an electronic digital computer called Colossus. This computer was based on vacuum tubes and was used for intelligence-related tasks including the Ultra project for deciphering German communications. This computer may have been the first "electronic" digital computer.

1.1.2 • Development of Computer Memory

Even though the idea of storing both data and programs in computer memory was proposed for the Edvac in 1946, the first computer to actually operate using this technique was the Manchester University (England) Mark I computer developed by Frederic C. Williams and Tom Kilburn in June, 1948. This computer utilized Cathode Ray Tube (CRT) storage, which was developed by Williams, and had an instruction cycle time of 1.2 milliseconds. The Williams storage tube had a capacity of thirty-two, 32-*bit* (binary digit) words.

Another stored program computer, the Edsac (Electronic Delay Storage Automatic Computer), was completed in 1949. Work began on Edsac in 1946 by Professor Maurice Wilkes of Cambridge University. Wilkes was familiar with the Edvac concept and utilized some similar ideas in the Edsac. For memory, Edsac used five-foot mercury delay lines.

Both the Manchester Mark I and the Cambridge Edsac were completed before the Edvac, which was finished in 1951. In the interim, Eckert and Mauchley left the University of Pennsylvania to establish their own computer company. Their first product was the Binac (Binary Automatic Computer), which was developed for Northrop Aircraft Company in 1950. Binac was a stored program computer that also used mercury delay lines for storage.

Back in 1944, the M.I.T. Servomechanism Laboratory also began working on project Whirlwind to develop electronic digital computers for flight simulation and pilot training. Whirlwind I was completed in March, 1951 and its components included 11,000 diodes and 5,000 vacuum tubes. Whirlwind used parallel data paths in contrast to some of the other computers that used serial paths. Whirlwind operated on 15-bit words. Jay W. Forrester, who was a principal in the Whirlwind project, applied the properties of magnetic cores to develop a computer memory and, in 1953, applied this memory to the Whirlwind computer.

1.1.3 • Commercial Expansion

The impetus and technology of the digital computer had now developed to the point where commercialization could expand. Ferranti Limited delivered the first commercial version of the Manchester Mark I in February, 1951. In the United States, the Remington Rand Corporation, by its acquisition of Eckert Mauchley Computer Corporation, became the biggest supplier of computers. Remington Rand delivered its Univac I (Universal Automatic Computer I) in June of 1951 to the U.S. Census Bureau. The Univac I was a serial machine that was built with 5,000 vacuum tubes, operated at a 2.25 Megahertz rate (2.25 million timing cycles per second), could store 1,000 12-digit decimal numbers, and used 100 mercury delay lines. A multiplication was performed in 2.5 milliseconds and an addition in 0.5 milliseconds. A notable characteristic of the Univac I was that it was the first to use metal-based magnetic tape for bulk storage.

The Univac 1103, utilizing magnetic core memory, was introduced in 1953 and was 50 times faster than the Univac I. Univac pioneered the move away from vacuum tubes to transistors. The Univac III, in 1960, introduced operating system software, which is a set of programs that allow a user to control the computer and its resources with relatively simple statements.

1.1.4 • IBM Contributions

One of IBM's earliest computers was the Selective Sequence Electronic Calculator introduced in 1948. This machine was composed of both relays and vacuum tubes (21,400 relays and 12,500 vacuum tubes). It operated on 19-digit numbers with an add time of 0.28 milliseconds. IBM introduced the model 701 computer in 1952. The IBM 701 was a parallel computer (one that processed its binary digits all at once in an operation) composed of 12,000 solid state (germanium) diodes and 4,000 vacuum tubes. The 701 used 36-bit words, added in 62.5 microseconds (millionths of a second), and multiplied in 50 milliseconds. Punched cards were used for input and output and 72 Williams storage tubes of 1,024 bits each made up the 2,048 word memory. The memory had a 12-microsecond cycle time (time to go through one cycle of a read or write operation).

IBM introduced a number of machines following the 701. These computers were the 702, 704, and 705. The 704 and 705 were introduced in 1954 and were followed by the IBM 650, which used disks similar to phonograph records for storage. Each disk could hold 1 million characters of data. IBM's transistor computer introduction occurred in 1958 with the IBM 7090 machine. In 1959, IBM introduced another transistorized machine, the model 1401, which became popular throughout the world.

1.1.5 • Development of Computer Languages

During 1956 and 1957, John Backus of IBM developed a Formula Translation compiler or FORTRAN compiler to make it easier to program the IBM 704 computer. A compiler is a program that "translates" other programs written in English-like formula notation into machine-understandable programs. Another attempt to assist in programming was the introduction in 1959 of ALGOL or algorithmic language. In 1960, the Navy introduced COBOL or Common Business Oriented Language. Languages such as FORTRAN, ALGOL, and COBOL are known as *high-level* or *high-order* languages.

1.1.6 • Other Companies' Contributions

In the fifties, other companies such as RCA, GE, Control Data, and Honeywell also entered the computer marketplace. RCA and GE were later to withdraw. Control Data Corporation was incorporated in July, 1956. The Control Data 1605 was designed by one of Control Data's founders, Seymour Cray, who also designed the small Control Data 160 in 1959.

1.1.7 • Development of the Minicomputer

Kenneth Olsen, who had worked on the Whirlwind project at M.I.T., paved the way for the minicomputer when he and some associates founded the Digital Equipment Corporation (DEC) in 1957. In 1959, Olsen used the Corporation's product line of semiconductor modules to implement the PDP–1 (Programmed Data Processor). The PDP–1 sold for approximately $120,000, which was an extremely low cost relative to other computers of the time.

Other "small-scale" computers, as they were referred to at the time, preceded the DEC PDP–1, but were not solid state (transistorized) machines. These computers included the Burroughs E–101, Bendix G–15, and the Librascope LGP–30 that was marketed by Royal-McBee. These computers manipulated data serially and used vacuum tubes and diodes. The E–101 also employed some stepping-switch logic and was externally programmed by physically inserting conductive pins in matrix boards. It used a nonexpandable magnetic drum memory with a capacity of 220 12-decimal-digit words. The E–101 had a typical add time of 5 milliseconds to add 2 12-decimal-digit numbers. The Bendix G–15 and the Librascope LGP–30 had similar add times, but stored programs along with data on their drum memories. The G–15 drum memory capacity was 2,176 29-bit words and the LGP–30 was 4,096 32-bit words. Interpretive languages (languages in which relatively complex instructions were executed by running preexisting small programs made up of a series of simpler instructions) were provided for these two machines to ease the programming tasks.

The Control Data 160 and the IBM 1620 were two small-scale solid state machines introduced circa 1959, 1960. The 1620 was a variable word length machine that performed the basic add function by table lookup. The CDC 160 had an add instruction time of 12.8 microseconds, utilized a parallel adder, had 12-bit instruction and data words, and had a memory capacity of 4K (kilo) words (4 thousand words).

Digital Equipment Corporation further advanced computer-based, "real-time" data acquisition and control in 1963 with the PDP–5 and its reimplementation, the PDP–8, in 1965. These 12-bit "minicomputers," as they were now called, used discrete transistor logic and employed core memory. The PDP–5 system that included 4K 12-bit words of core memory and a teleprinter with paper tape input/output sold for the incredibly low price of $30,000. The PDP–5 add time was 18 microseconds while that of the PDP–8 was 3.2 microseconds. The cost of the PDP–8 was $18,000. For the "real-time" applications, the PDP–5/8 provided hardware program interrupt, a real-time clock, and Direct Memory Access (DMA) that enabled direct, rapid transfer of data to and from computer memory relative to external devices. This direct connection, which essentially bypassed the processor, made possible data transfers of 625,000 words per second—about four times faster than input/output under program control. The PDP–8 also had a software library that included a FORTRAN compiler that ran in less than 8K words of memory.

Also, in the latter part of 1965, the 16-bit minicomputer was introduced. These machines were developed principally by Computer Control Company; Data Machines, Inc.; and IBM. Computer Control Company introduced the DDP–116 that later became the Honeywell 316, 416, and 516 through acquisition. Similarly, the Data Machines 620 became the Varian Data Machines 620i, 620f, 620l, and V–73. The IBM computers introduced were the 1800 for system control and a variation, the 1130, for scientific computation. The computers from all three companies were expandable, general purpose machines, used core memory, incorporated some integrated circuits, were aimed at real-time data acquisition and control, and provided FORTRAN compiler software support.

1.1.8 • More Developments

In the large computer class, IBM introduced the System 360 compatible family of computers in April, 1964. This line of computers consisted of six models—the 30, 40, 50, 60, 62, and 70. A model 85, which ushered in cache memory (high-speed memory in which programs retrieved from slower, mass storage devices could be stored and later executed), was introduced. Operating system programs to manage the computer and its associated resources for the System 360 were the DOS (Disk Operating System) for the small-to-medium machines and the OS/360 (Operating System 360) for the large computers. The System 360 line was built of Solid Logic, which was *hybrid circuitry*. Hybrid circuitry utilized a number of integrated circuit chips interconnected on a common substrate. In 1970, System 370 was introduced. These computers and associated memory were built of monolithic integrated circuits that were circuits implemented on a single chip.

Other competitive computer introductions during the early 1960's were the Sperry Rand 1107 in 1962 and the 1108 in 1964. Sperry Rand also introduced the Univac models 9200 and 9300 in 1966.

Innovations such as *multiprogramming* (multiple programs running concurrently on a single computer) and *virtual memory* (appearance of external mass memory such as disks as almost unlimited program memory available to the processor for execution) appeared in the Burroughs B5000 in 1961. Updated versions of this machine were the B5500 introduced in 1964 and the B2500, B3500, and B6500 in 1966. The B2500 and B3500 used monolithic integrated circuits in their construction. The B6500 featured multiprogramming, parallel processing, and timesharing. Control Data Incorporated introduced two supercomputers, models 6600 in 1963 and 7600 in 1968.

At this point, the stage was set for the evolution of the microprocessor. Progress in semiconductor processing technology was the driving force that integrated the processor onto a single silicon chip. Let us trace the evolution of the microprocessor through the historical development of semiconductor technology.

1.2 • EVOLUTION OF THE MICROPROCESSOR

A high point in the development of semiconductor technology, which eventually made the microprocessor possible, was the invention of the transistor at Bell Laboratories on December 23, 1947. This device, which then consisted of gold foil contacts on a slab of germanium, was invented by John Bardeen, Walter Brattain, and William Shockley, who were awarded the Nobel Prize in physics for this work in 1956. The transistor made it possible to switch electrical circuits and amplify electrical signals in small, low-power devices. With new and improved methods of creating semiconductor junctions emerging in the 1950's, the transistor was applied in military products and, later, in consumer products.

1.2.1 • The Integrated Circuit

Another milestone was reached in 1959 when a complete circuit was integrated onto a wafer. This advance was accomplished independently and almost simultaneously by Jack Kilby of Texas Instruments and Robert Noyce of Fairchild Semiconductor. For the first time, an integrated circuit containing active and passive components was placed on a single chip of semiconductor material. The transistors developed and used in these innovations up to this time were *bipolar transistors*. Bipolar transistors utilize current composed of both positive and negative charges (hence the name bipolar) and consume relatively large amounts of power.

Another type of transistor, the field effect transistor or FET, was patented at RCA Laboratories, in 1957. This type of transistor, which was the subject of experiments about 20 years earlier at Bell Laboratories, operates on low currents and thus can be made much smaller than bipolar devices. It was a version of the FET, the MOSFET (a Metal Oxide Semiconductor FET) that made possible the high-density integrated circuits of today. This device, which was also developed at RCA in 1962, operates on very low currents since the gate that controls current flow in the transistor is insulated from the transistor substrate.

Processing of the MOSFET was more difficult than that of the bipolar transistor, and this delayed its development during the 1960's. By the late 1960's, MOSFET technology had advanced to the point where high-density devices were possible.

1.2.2 • The First Generation of Microprocessors

In 1969, Intel Corporation was requested by Busicom Corporation of Japan to develop integrated circuits for calculators. Marcian E. Hoff, Intel's manager of application research, proposed a single chip processor with support chips to provide read/write random access memory (RAM), read only memory (ROM) for non-volatile program storage, and input/output (I/O). This chip set was designed by Federico Faggin (who later was cofounder and president of Zilog, Inc.) and was announced in 1971 as the MCS 4004 microprocessor chip set. In addition to the 4004 processor, the chip set comprised the 4001 256 *byte* (8-bit) ROM with I/O, the 4002 32-bit RAM with I/O, and the 4003 10-bit shift register.

In late 1971 and early 1972, Stan Mazor and Mike Markula of Intel traveled around the country introducing the MCS 4004 family to industry.

Shortly after the design of the 4004, Computer Terminals Corporation (later to become Datapoint) requested that Intel develop a chip to support their new terminal design. The resulting product was the Intel 8008 processor, which, because of certain design changes, was not used by Computer Terminals Corporation. The 8008 was the first commercial eight-bit microprocessor and was introduced in early 1972. The 8008 provided 45 instructions, was in an 18-pin package, and sold for $200 in 1972.

In 1973, Rockwell introduced the PPS–4 four-bit microprocessor and National Semiconductor developed its GPCP (General Purpose Controller/Processor). This device was a *bit slice* design that was a "slice" of a microprocessor. Slices could be concatenated to create a machine of up to 32 bits in word length.

1.2.3 • Continued Microprocessor Development

Second generation microprocessors were introduced in 1974 with the eight-bit Intel 8080 and the eight-bit Motorola 6800 devices. The 8080 was upwardly compatible with the 8008, but had four times the memory address space (64K). Using the Intel devices as an example, upward compatibility means that programs that ran on the 8008 could also execute on the 8080, but the reverse condition would not be true. The 8080 was designed by Masatoshi

Shima who eventually went to Zilog to design the Z80. Shima later returned to work for Intel in his own laboratory in Japan.

The Motorola 6800 bus structure was similar to that of the PDP–11 and was supported by compatible interface chips such as the 6810 128-byte static RAM, 6816 ROM, 6820 peripheral interface adapter (PIA), and the 6850 asynchronous communications interface adapter (ACIA). Also, in 1974, National Semiconductor introduced its PACE (Processing and Control Element) 16-bit microprocessor. In 1976, Texas Instruments brought out the TI 9900 16-bit microprocessor that offered instruction set compatibility upward to TI minicomputers. In the same year, Intel introduced the 8048 single chip microcomputer that, in addition to the processor, contained RAM, ROM, I/O, interval timing, and pulse counting on a single chip.

1.2.4 • Maturing Microprocessor Technology

With the ability to integrate more transistors onto a silicon chip, semiconductor manufacturers began to address systems considerations. High among these considerations was the ability to handle analog information on a digital chip. In 1978, Intel introduced the 8022 single chip microcomputer that had two analog inputs. Also, in the same year, Intel introduced the 2920 signal processing device that had both analog inputs and outputs.

As for computational power, 1978 saw the introduction of the next generation "designed-with-software-in-mind," minicomputer-like, 16-bit microcomputer systems. The most prominent of these were the Motorola 68000, Zilog Z8000, and the Intel 8086. The 68000, for example, is a 16-bit microprocessor that is, internally, actually a 32-bit device. Its design incorporates instructions to support high-level languages, operating systems, and parallel processing with multiple microprocessors.

A fourth generation microcomputer that further emphasizes this trend toward large machine performance and high-level language support is the Intel 432 32-bit micromainframe system. This system is more powerful than many existing minicomputers and provides extensive on-chip implementation of language, operating system, and multiprocessing support features. The 432 system basic components, excluding memory, are the iAPX 43201 instruction decode unit, the iAPX 43202 instruction execution unit, and the iAPX 43203 interface processor unit. The iAPX 43201 and iAPX 43202 chips make up the 32-bit 432 General Data Processor or GDP. The 43201 instruction decode unit is composed of 100,000 active devices (transistors) integrated onto a silicon wafer, while the 43202 and 43203 chips are made up of 60,000 such active devices. As a basis of comparison, the number of transistors on the Intel 43201 chip is roughly 5 times the number on the Intel 8086 16-bit microprocessor chip. For relative instruction execution speed, the 432 runs at approximately 0.25 million instructions per second (*mips*), the Intel 8086 at 0.2 mips, the Digital Equipment Corporation (DEC) PDP 11/34 minicomputer at 0.2 mips, the DEC VAX 11/780 32-bit super minicomputer at 1 mips, and the IBM 370/158 large computer at 2 mips. Volume-wise, the 432 central processor (including chassis and power supply but excluding memory) would occupy approximately 2 cubic feet as compared to 1 cubic foot for the 8086, 9 cubic feet for the DEC PDP 11/34, 185 cubic feet for the DEC VAX 11/780, and 600 cubic feet for the IBM 370/158.

Since the 432 is typical of the new generation of micromainframes, it may be helpful to list a few of its features. The following are especially noteworthy: the capability of adding processors to the 432 system to extend performance, provision of software support for this multiprocessing, incorporation of operating system and fault-tolerant facilities in its design, and the inclusion of support for Ada, the DoD standard high-level language. In this regard, hardware and software systems aimed at utilizing and supporting Ada will be in demand in the 1980's. Ada is based on Pascal and is effective in real-time applications and environments utilizing concurrent processing. The language was named after countess Ada Lovelace, the daughter of Lord Byron. Countess Lovelace was an assistant to nineteenth-century mathematician Charles Babbage, and for her contributions in that capacity, she is sometimes referred to as the "first computer programmer."

1.3 • ECONOMIC IMPACT OF THE MICROPROCESSOR

Before the introduction of the microprocessor in 1971, the total number of computers in the world was approximately 200,000. If one considers that one semiconductor company can turn out more than 50,000 microcomputers each month, some impact on society and the economy is, at least, highly probable. The fact that computational power is now available in high volume, at low cost, with relatively small power consumption, and in small physical size means that there is a tremendous potential for replacing traditionally mechanical systems and enhancing existing electronic systems. From adding machines to calculators, from personal record books to personal computers—the microprocessor has already eradicated markets for many traditional products and created demands for items that did not exist less than five years ago. The microprocessor itself is a mainline product for many companies that were not in existence 10 years ago.

1.3.1 • Relationship of Volume to Cost

Figure 1.2 is the traditional semiconductor industry learning curve showing that for each doubling of the cumulative volume of a semiconductor product, say a microprocessor, the cost of the product is reduced by 27% (see next page).

This curve, which holds in general, points out a company's advantage in bringing a successful semiconductor device to market before a competitor. With a lead in volume production of the product, the company introducing the device can take advantage of learning curve cost reductions against a late-starting competitor for the same market. In the very early stages of a product's lifetime, the manufacturer can also charge a high price if there is no comparable competitive device available.

Some products, such as Texas Instruments' TMS 1000 single-chip microcomputer introduced in 1974, have traversed the learning curve to such an extent that they sell for less than a dollar in

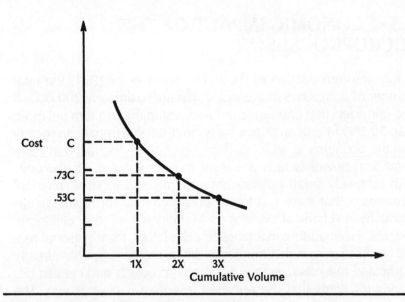

Figure 1.2 Semiconductor Learning Curve

volume. With microcomputers available at such low cost, and similar products continually working their way down the learning curve, computing capability will permeate the home and work-place.

Since volume is the key to low price for microcomputers and for semiconductor devices in general, high-volume products such as automobiles, TV sets, games, calculators, appliances, point-of-sale terminals, and personal computers have been the initial targets of microcomputer application. Other areas that hold promise are telephone and related items, home video recorders, home thermostats and security systems, and TV-text facilities offering in-home document retrieval, news, stock quotations, and the like.

1.3.2 • Programming Cost Reduction

The low cost of microcomputers is made possible by high volume production. Unfortunately, programming of the micro-computer is still labor-intensive and, thus, a high cost item. Assuming an average programmer productivity rate of 10 lines of debugged code per day (which is, in fact, high according to numerous studies), a 1,000-line program would take approximately 100 days or 800 hours to write, debug, and have running. For a programmer earning $15 per hour, the programming cost would be $12,000. A fully burdened cost including benefits and overhead would be even higher, perhaps at a level of $25,000 or more.

Amortization of the software costs over a large number of items is an obvious means of reducing the per unit cost of software development.

The traditional objective in software development for microcomputers was to "pack the code tightly" in order to minimize the amount of memory required to hold the code. Since memory costs have been plummeting and higher density memories are now available in single chips (64K bits to 1M bit), this objective is becoming secondary in most cases to the reduction of the labor-intensive software development costs. It is in this context that the use of high-level languages is now becoming popular for use in programming microcomputers. These languages permit programmers to develop codes using English-like statements and algebraic formulas that are familiar and understandable to others who will later have to utilize, maintain, or modify the software.

Since instructions in this form are not recognizable by the microcomputer, another program, a *compiler*, is required for a one-to-many translation of the high-level statements to the simple binary representations of *machine language* required by the microcomputer. Since this compilation process is usually inefficient, more machine language instructions are generated than would be produced by an experienced programmer writing in *assembly language*. Assembly language instructions correspond one-to-one with the binary machine language instructions of the microcomputer, and *mnemonics* or memory aids are used to represent these machine language instructions. For example, the machine language binary representation of an instruction to add two numbers may be 10001111, and the corresponding assembly language mnemonic may be ADD. The use of high-level languages such as FORTRAN, Pascal, PL/M, BASIC, and Ada for microcomputers can therefore reduce programming labor costs; but this is at the expense of requiring more memory to hold the compiler itself and the compiler-generated machine language code.

1.3.3 • Microprocessors and Industry

The economic impact of microprocessors will also be felt in the factory and processing plants. Microprocessors make it possible to have localized data acquisition and control throughout the plant. This was not previously economically feasible. Today, competitive pressures from foreign manufacturers are mandating increased productivity through automation and robotics while achieving higher levels of quality control. The microprocessor can ensure increased quality at each step of a production line, building quality "in" as an integral part of the manufacturing process, so that product sampling at different stages becomes unnecessary.

Making local, microprocessor-based intelligent terminals available to each professional employee of an organization can radically change the office environment. Correspondence among personnel and supervisors can take place by computer mail to respective terminals. Input into word processing stations can be taken from draft files developed by individuals using editing and formatting programs at their personal terminals. Communication among individuals can be immediate, paper shuffling reduced, and office productivity increased.

In short, placing the intelligence in the form of programmed microcomputers at the point of greatest potential impact on an operation is now and will continue to be economically and technically feasible. In this way, existing deficiencies and inefficiencies in operation can be eliminated or reduced, resulting in more competitive plants yielding high outputs of quality products. For many industries, such as steel and automobile manufacturing, this approach is not only desirable, but it may be the key to survival.

1.4 • TRENDS AND FUTURE CONSIDERATIONS

Extrapolating the developments outlined in this chapter into the decade of the 1980's, some interesting observations can be offered.

From the computer industry viewpoint, the trend toward *distributed processing* will continue. In this context, distributed processing does not mean intelligent terminals and remote computers communicating with larger central machines, but refers to multiple, independent computers with their own programs and memory operating cooperatively toward a common goal. In this definition, no single computer is master over the others, but control is distributed among all the computers in the system. A good example of distributed control is a baseball team on the field. There is no one person directly controlling the movement of each player when the ball is hit, but they work together without central control toward the common goal of putting out the batter or base runner.

The microcomputer is the ideal component of a distributed computing system. A distributed microcomputer system, when achieved, can have the computing capability of a super computer at a fraction of the cost. Such a system, properly designed, can have its computing capability increased by the addition of other microcomputers. Advantages in maintenance, reliability, and survivability can also be achieved in a distributed system.

In the software arena, more programs will reside in the microprocessor itself, since the density of integration will continue to increase and large amounts of memory can occupy the same silicon chip as the processor. In addition to software for performing arithmetic and trigonometric functions, programs for controlling external resources such as printers, disk storage, and so on will reside in the microprocessor chip. As seen in the previously described Intel 432 micromainframe, software for controlling multiple processors and providing some level of fault tolerance have already become a part of the microprocessor chip. Furthermore, compilers for high-level languages such as Ada and Pascal will reside in the chip memory.

Such conglomerates of resource control programs, administrative recordkeeping, arithmetic support, and compilers are called operating system programs or *operating systems*. In addition to operating systems residing on the microprocessor chip, future high-integration levels will begin to incorporate speech recognition, speech output, and some forms of artificial intelligence. The ramifications of such capabilities on automation, control, home data banks, communications, transportation, and work habits are obvious. The important thing to remember is that such developments are no longer laboratory curiosities; they are already being designed into commercial products.

Because of the rapid and continuing progress in fitting more and more transistors onto a single silicon chip (presently about 100K on the commercial level as shown in the Intel 432), the problem that exists now for the semiconductor industry is *what* to put on the chip. Recall that, except for military needs, the parts must sell in high volume to be affordable by the product consumer. Since microprocessors normally require from 6K to 60K transistors (excluding micromainframes), what other systems can be integrated onto silicon? We have seen that developing computer memory to hold large amounts of software is one solution. Other solutions must face the critical issue that the more complex a device is, the less universal it is. The less universal it is, the more difficult it is to sell in volume. The microprocessor, customized by programming, is one complex product meeting the requirements of density and universality. Other alternatives are scarce.

Bibliography

Bell, C.G., and Newell, A. *Computer Structures: Readings and Examples.* New York: McGraw-Hill, Inc., 1971.

"Description of the Relay Calculator." *Annals of the Harvard Computation Labs,* vol. 24. Cambridge, Mass.: Harvard University Press, 1949.

Electronics. New York: McGraw-Hill, Inc., April 17, 1980.

Intel Corporation. *Intel MCS-40 Users Manual,* March 1975, pp. iii–x.

Koudela, J., Jr. "The Past, Present, and Future of Minicomputers: A Scenario." *Proceedings of the IEEE,* vol. 61, no. 11, November 1973, pp. 1526–1534.

Krutz, R.L. *Microprocessors and Logic Design.* New York: John Wiley and Sons, Inc., 1980.

Turing, A.M. "On Computable Numbers with an Application to the Entscheidungsproblem." *Proceedings of the London Mathematical Society,* vol. 42, no. 2, 1936–1937, pp. 230–265.

Chapter Two

FUNDAMENTAL DIGITAL BUILDING BLOCKS

2.1 • BACKGROUND

Far from being an overnight development, the microprocessor is simply a composition of previously existing "building blocks" packed into an area roughly 0.2 inches by 0.2 inches. Its breakthrough coincides with the discovery of a way to integrate these building blocks, or circuits, onto a silicon chip. This chapter covers microprocessor building blocks from a functional point of view in terms of the inputs to the blocks and the resulting outputs. The treatment is meant to be appropriate for managers and is not intended to be a detailed treatise of digital logic. The terminology of binary devices is presented to prepare the reader for discussions of basic logic functions, storage elements, and arithmetic functions. At the end of the chapter, the typical microprocessor is illustrated and discussed in terms of a block diagram, utilizing the "building blocks" concept discussed here.

2.2 • BINARY STATE REPRESENTATIONS

Since the transistor, which is equivalent to the atomic structure of the microprocessor or memory, operates in a binary or two-state mode in digital systems, the symbols 1 and 0 are assigned to these states. The transistor operates as a switch, either "ON" and conducting current or "OFF" and not conducting current. The symbol 1 can be assigned to one of these states and the symbol 0 to the other, as long as they are applied consistently.

With only two states capable of being reliably indicated by a transistor, any numbers or instructions to be held in the microprocessor or associated memory must be represented by multiple transistors producing combinations of the binary states. Thus the binary number system, which has only two allowable digits (1 and 0), is used in digital computers—and not the familiar decimal system, which has ten legal digits (0 through 9). By interpreting the 1 and 0 states of the transistors as the binary numbers or binary digits *(bits)* 1 and 0, the microprocessor can store instructions and data.

In order to interpret the number represented by the bits 1 and 0, each digit in the binary number is assigned a weight, exactly as done in the decimal system. Take the decimal number 9612 for example. In interpreting this number, we implicitly assign weights to each digit as follows:

$$\frac{1000}{9} \quad \frac{100}{6} \quad \frac{10}{1} \quad \frac{1}{2} \quad \longleftarrow \quad \text{weights}$$

The number 2 is assigned a weight of 1, so its value is 2 × 1 or 2. The digit 1 is assigned a weight of 10, so its value is 1 × 10 or 10. The digits 6 and 9 are assigned the weights of 100 and 1000 respectively, yielding values of 6 × 100 or 600 and 9 × 1000 or 9000. The total value of the number representation 9612 is, then

$$9000 + 600 + 10 + 2 \qquad \text{or}$$

nine thousand six hundred and twelve

The interpretation of a binary number takes place in the same manner except that the weights are powers of 2, instead of powers of 10. Remembering that there are only two permissible digits, 1 and 0, in the *binary system*, let us interpret the binary number 1101 using binary weights.

$$\frac{8}{1} \quad \frac{4}{1} \quad \frac{2}{0} \quad \frac{1}{1} \quad \longleftarrow \quad \text{weights}$$

Using the same technique as in the decimal case, the binary number 1101 is equivalent to

$$1 \times 8 + 1 \times 4 + 0 \times 2 + 1 \times 1 \qquad \text{or}$$

$$13$$

in decimal form. In order to distinguish a binary number from a decimal number that has only 1's and 0's in it, a subscript is used. For example, the number 1101_2 represents a binary number equivalent to a decimal 13, while the number 1101 represents the decimal number "one thousand, one hundred, and one."

All addition, multiplication, subtraction, and so on are performed in the microprocessor using binary numbers. Translation to this form from the familiar decimal form is done by a program residing in the microprocessor that is part of the assembler or compiler. To add the numbers 5 and 3 in binary, the microprocessor would perform the following operation:

$$
\begin{array}{ll}
1\ 1 & \\
1\ 0\ 1 & (+5) \\
\underline{+\ \ 0\ 1\ 1} & \underline{(+3)} \\
1\ 0\ 0\ 0 & (\ \ 8)
\end{array}
$$

Note that a carry is generated out of the binary addition of $1 + 1$ and propagates down to each column.

Microprocessors operate on binary numbers of lengths up to 32 bits. This many 1's and 0's are difficult to work with and interpret from the human point of view. When the user must deal with numbers in the 1 and 0 realm, a shorthand notation called *hexadecimal* or base 16 is applied. It is an easy method to use and understand, since it is analogous to the binary (base 2) and decimal (base 10) systems previously discussed.

As the binary or base 2 system has two digits, 0 and 1, and the decimal or base 10 system has 10 digits, 0 through 9, the hexadecimal or base 16 system has 16 digits. Since we run out of conventional single symbols for digits after 9, the letters A through F are used as the single symbols for the numbers 10 through 15, respectively. The digits of the hexadecimal number system and their decimal equivalents are summarized in Table 2.1.

Table 2.1 Hexadecimal Digits and Their Decimal Equivalents

Hex Digits	Decimal Equivalent
0	0
1	1
2	2
3	3
4	4
5	5
6	6
7	7
8	8
9	9
A	10
B	11
C	12
D	13
E	14
F	15

As previously discussed with the binary and decimal number systems, a hexadecimal number can be converted to its decimal equivalent by interpreting each hexadecimal digit as a power of 16. For example, the hexadecimal number A08F can be interpreted as:

$$\frac{4096}{A} \quad \frac{256}{0} \quad \frac{16}{8} \quad \frac{1}{F} \quad \longleftarrow \quad \text{weights}$$

$$A \times 4096 + 0 \times 256 + 8 \times 16 + F \times 1 =$$

$$10 \times 4096 + 0 \times 256 + 8 \times 16 + 15 \times 1 =$$

$$40,960 + 0 + 128 + 15 = 41,103$$

Thus, we can write

$$A08F_{16} = 41,103_{10}$$

With this background, we can use the hexadecimal notation as a shorthand for long binary numbers. The binary number 1101001100011010 can be converted to the hex number D31A by taking the bits in groups of four, beginning from the right, and interpreting each group, individually, as a hexadecimal number. Illustrating this technique with the example binary number yields:

1101	0011	0001	1010
D	3	1	A

With this method, a 16-bit decimal number can be represented by a 4-digit hexadecimal number. The reverse of this method can also be used. If a location in the memory of a 16-bit address microprocessor is given as 00FF, the binary pattern 0000000011111111 will be sent out from the microprocessor to the memory. This binary number is obtained by reversing the procedure given in the previous example.

0	0	F	F
0000	0000	1111	1111

The hex notation can also be used to represent instructions. If a hypothetical microprocessor has an ADD instruction represented by the pattern 11110111, the hexadecimal code F7 can be used as a short form to identify the instruction.

In order to complete this discussion of binary representations, negative numbers must be considered. The microprocessor, or any processor for that matter, must have a way of distinguishing positive numbers from negative numbers. The most widely used method of representing negative numbers in binary is the *two's complement* form. To find the negative of a number in binary form, the two's complement of the number is taken.

There are two common ways to do this. The first is to *complement* each bit in the binary number (complement means to change a 0 to a 1 and 1 to a 0) and add a 1 to the result. As an example, let's use this method to calculate the two's complement of the binary number 0011. Complementing 0011 produces 1100. Adding a 1 to this result yields 1101. Note the leftmost bit or *most significant bit* (msb) of the two's complement is a 1. In two's complement notation, a binary number having a 1 in the most significant bit position is defined as being negative. The msb is referred to as the *sign bit*. Since the msb is used to represent the sign, it is not available to represent the magnitude of the number. The following is a number line showing the positive and negative numbers represented by three bits and a sign bit (four bits total). As noted earlier, the msb of the negative numbers is always a 1.

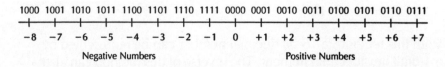

1000 1001 1010 1011 1100 1101 1110 1111	0000 0001 0010 0011 0100 0101 0110 0111
−8 −7 −6 −5 −4 −3 −2 −1	0 +1 +2 +3 +4 +5 +6 +7
Negative Numbers	Positive Numbers

Another way to find the two's complement of a binary number is to copy each digit of the binary number sequentially from the right until the first 1 is encountered. Copy the first 1 and complement each remaining digit individually. The following example uses this technique to find the two's complement of 00110100.

complement all remaining	00110 | 100	copy digits from
digits individually after	|	right up to and
first 1	11001 | 100	including first 1

Thus, 11001100 is the two's complement of 00110100.

2.3 • LOGIC AND ARITHMETIC FUNCTIONS

Transistors fabricated in an integrated circuit can be used to create logic functions, storage elements, and arithmetic functions. In this section, logic and arithmetic functions will be examined with discussions of storage functions to follow in subsequent sections.

There are seven basic combinational logic functions. A combinational logic function can be defined as a binary function whose output is determined by the combination of inputs and not the sequence in which they are applied. The seven basic combinational logic functions are the AND, OR, NOT (INVERT), NAND, NOR, EXCLUSIVE OR, and EXCLUSIVE NOR (coincidence). These functions can be simply defined by tables showing the combinations of possible 1 and 0 inputs and the corresponding outputs. Such tables are known as *tables of combinations*. Tables of combinations for the seven combinational logic functions with two inputs are given in Figure 2.1 on the following page.

The symbols for each function are given with the corresponding table. A and B are input lines while T is the output line. Typically 1's and 0's are represented by voltages in actual circuits. For example, a 1 could be approximately 2.5 volts and a 0 could be 0 volts.

As seen in the tables, an AND circuit has its output equal to 1 only when both inputs (A and B) are equal to a 1. Similarly, an OR circuit has a 1 output when either input (A or B) or both are equal to a 1. A NOT function simply inverts the input while NAND and NOR circuits are AND and OR circuits whose outputs are inverted (NOT AND and NOT OR). Circuits performing logic functions are sometimes called *gates*. Thus, an EXCLUSIVE OR gate has its output equal to a 1 when either but not both of its inputs are equal to a 1. An EXCLUSIVE NOR or coincidence gate is the same as an EXCLUSIVE OR gate whose output is inverted and has a 1 output when both inputs are identical. EXCLUSIVE OR and EXCLUSIVE NOR circuits are used to compare two binary numbers and for addition and subtraction operations. In fact, any of the more complex logic circuits can be made from the seven basic combinational circuits. Some of the common combinational logic circuits used in microprocessor implementations will now be discussed.

2.3.1 • Full Adder

A full adder is a fundamental addition circuit that adds two bits and a "carry in" from a previous stage and produces a sum

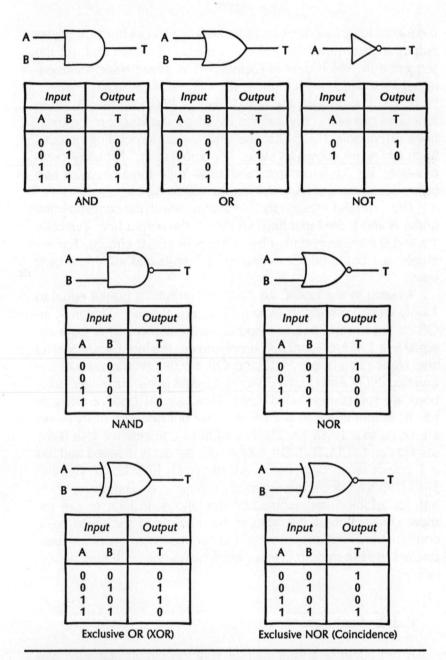

Figure 2.1 Tables of Combinations of Basic Logic Functions

bit and a "carry out" to the next stage. Arithmetically, the operation is

$$\text{bit A} + \text{bit B} + \text{carry in} = \text{sum bit with carry out}$$

For example, if bit A = 1, bit B = 0, and carry in = 1, the full adder would implement

$$
\begin{array}{rl}
1 & \text{(carry in)} \\
1 & \text{(A)} \\
+\ 0 & \text{(B)} \\
\hline
\text{(carry out)}\quad 10 & \text{(sum)}
\end{array}
$$

The block diagram of a full adder is shown in Figure 2.2.

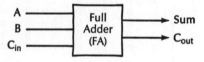

Figure 2.2 Full Adder

2.3.2 • Decoder

A decoder activates a particular output line for each possible combination of binary inputs. The table of combinations and block diagram for a three-input decoder are given in Figure 2.3 (p. 30). Note that only one of the eight output lines is active at one time. A decoder of this type is called a three-to-eight decoder, signifying that a unique output line is activated corresponding to each of the eight possible input combinations of three bits. From this discussion, it can be seen that, in a binary system, there are 2^n possible combinations of the 1's and 0's that make up an n-bit number.

2.3.3 • Arithmetic Logic Unit

The arithmetic logic unit or ALU is a key component of the microprocessor. This element performs arithmetic and logic func-

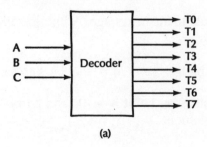

(a)

Input			Output							
A	B	C	T0	T1	T2	T3	T4	T5	T6	T7
0	0	0	1	0	0	0	0	0	0	0
0	0	1	0	1	0	0	0	0	0	0
0	1	0	0	0	1	0	0	0	0	0
0	1	1	0	0	0	1	0	0	0	0
1	0	0	0	0	0	0	1	0	0	0
1	0	1	0	0	0	0	0	1	0	0
1	1	0	0	0	0	0	0	0	1	0
1	1	1	0	0	0	0	0	0	0	1

(b)

Figure 2.3 (a) Three-Input Decoder
(b) Table of Combinations

tions as its name implies. A typical ALU has two groups of input data lines, input control lines to specify the operations to be performed on the data, and output lines for the results. Figure 2.4 is a block diagram of a four-bit ALU.

In this ALU, A0–A3 and B0–B3 are input data lines. For example, they could be two binary numbers to be added. The lines F0–F4 specify the operations to be performed on the data, and outputs S0–S3 present the results. C_i or carry in line accepts a carry out from a previous ALU stage and C_o is the carry out from a summation operation. The A = B output indicates that a comparison of A and B inputs has shown them to be equal.

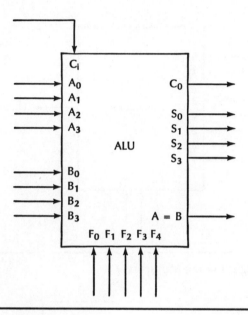

Figure 2.4 ALU Block Diagram

2.3.4 • Multiplexer

A digital multiplexer routes one of many input lines to a single output. The input line selected to be "connected" to the output line is specified by a number of select lines. An eight-to-one multiplexer is shown in Figure 2.5 on the next page. The line or channel to be selected for routing to the output is determined by the binary pattern placed on the select lines S0–S2. For example, 011 placed on select lines S0–S2 will connect input line 3 to the output.

2.3.5 • Demultiplexer

A demultiplexer is essentially the opposite of a multiplexer. It takes one input and routes it to one of many outputs as specified by the select inputs. In the diagram shown in Figure 2.6, a 101 on select lines S0–S2 will connect the input to output line 5.

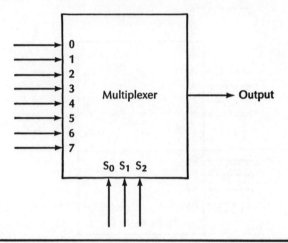

Figure 2.5 Eight-to-One Multiplexer

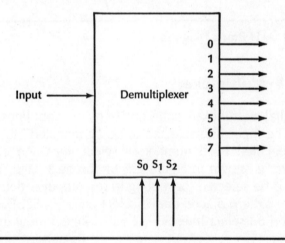

Figure 2.6 Demultiplexer

2.4 • STORAGE AND COUNTING ELEMENTS

In addition to combinational logic circuits, there are *sequential logic* circuits whose output depends not only upon the combination of inputs applied, but on the order or sequence in which they are applied. The most common types of sequential circuits utilized in microprocessors are storage and counting devices.

The basic storage device is the *flip-flop*. In contrast to a combinational circuit whose output corresponds to the input combination at any instant, the flip-flop can respond to a momentary input and remember that the input occurred. There are many different types of flip-flops, and one popular version, the JK flip-flop, is shown in Figure 2.7.

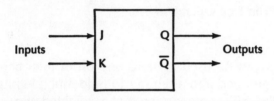

Figure 2.7 JK Flip-Flop

The J and K inputs can either have 1's or 0's on them and the outputs Q and $\overline{Q}$ can be 1's or 0's with the restriction that Q and $\overline{Q}$ are complementary. This means that if Q is a 1, then $\overline{Q}$ must be a 0 and vice versa. If a 1 is applied to the J input, either constantly or for a brief period of time (even microseconds or millionths of a second) while the K input is a 0, Q will be at a 1 state and $\overline{Q}$ will be a 0. Thus, if Q was initially a 0 and a transient 1 appeared on the J input while K was at a 0, Q would then be at a 1 level. The 1 would remain on Q (and a 0 on $\overline{Q}$) until the flip-flop was reset. One means of resetting the flip-flop is to reverse the previously described procedure between J and K. This reversal would entail placing a 1 on the K input while holding a 0 on the J input. This would "reset" Q to a 0 and $\overline{Q}$ to a 1. If a 1 was applied to both J and K simultaneously, the Q output would switch to a 1 if it was previously a 0 or to 0 if it was previously a 1. Figure 2.8 (see next page) summarizes the operation of the JK flip-flop.

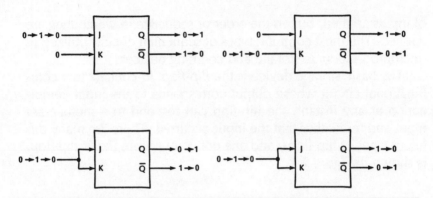

Figure 2.8 JK Flip-Flop Operation

Each flip-flop can be used to store one bit of information. Flip-flops can be grouped into a *register* to hold multiple bits. A four-bit register whose bit contents represent a weighted, binary number is shown in Figure 2.9.

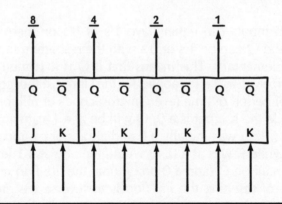

Figure 2.9 Four-Bit Register of JK Flip-Flops

For brevity, details of the flip-flops are usually omitted in a diagram. For example, Figure 2.10 is an eight-bit register with the msb on the left.

128	64	32	16	8	4	2	1

Figure 2.10 Eight-Bit Register

Another variation of the flip-flop is the *latch*. A latch usually has one data input line, a clock input line, and Q and $\overline{Q}$ outputs. The latch operates in such a way that a 0 or 1 present on the input data line is transferred to the Q output whenever the clock is applied. As before, $\overline{Q}$ is always the complement of the Q output. A latch, therefore, can be thought of as storing a 0 or 1 upon the application of a clock pulse, or a *strobe* pulse as it is sometimes called. Latches also are grouped so as to store multiple bits at a time. A one-bit latch and an eight-bit latch are shown in Figure 2.11.

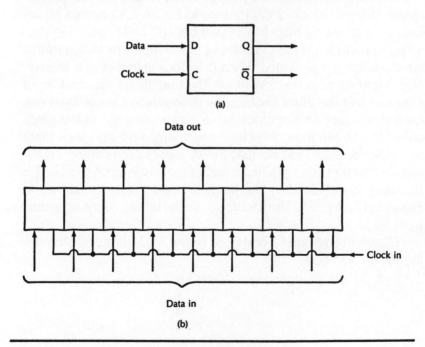

Figure 2.11 (a) One-Bit Latch, (b) Eight-Bit Latch

The clocked input used by the latch is also used with the JK and other types of flip-flops to make many varieties of flip-flops and, by adding of other logic elements, shifting and counting circuits.

A *shift register* simply moves a string of bits either to the left or right. For example, the bits 1101 shifted one position to the right would be 0110 with the msb filled in by a 0. Similarly, the same binary number shifted one position to the left would result in 1010 with the lsb, *least significant bit,* filled in by a 0. The shifting is usually accomplished by the application of a shift (clock) pulse to the register. Many varieties of shift registers are in use, some of which feed the bit shifted out of one end of the register into the other end (rotate). Also, data can be entered into the shift register flip-flops simultaneously (in parallel) and shifted out serially. Some examples are given in Figure 2.12.

A *counter* is composed of a number of flip-flops whose outputs (Q or $\overline{Q}$) taken collectively proceed through a repetitive sequence of patterns when activated by input count (clock) pulses. For example, the two clocked JK flip-flops in Figure 2.13 form a binary counter that counts from binary numbers 00 to 11 (0 to 3 in decimal). The circle on the clock input of the flip-flops indicates that the JK inputs are activated when the clock signal is at a 0 level. This is termed an *active low input.* The triangle on the clock input indicates that the clock enables the JK inputs to change from one level to another on the clock pulse, or on an edge of the clock pulse. In combination, the circle and triangle on the clock input of the JK flip-flop indicate that the JK inputs are enabled on the high to low transition (trailing edge) of the clock input signal. This transition is indicated by the shading in the waveform shown in Figure 2.13 on p. 38. The Q outputs are the binary counting pattern from 00 to 11.

Observing outputs Q_x and Q_y in Figure 2.13, they cycle through the binary numbers — — — ———

$$
\begin{array}{cc}
0 & 0 \\
0 & 1 \\
1 & 0 \\
1 & 1 \\
\end{array}
$$

— — — ———

$$
\begin{array}{cc}
0 & 0 \\
\end{array}
$$

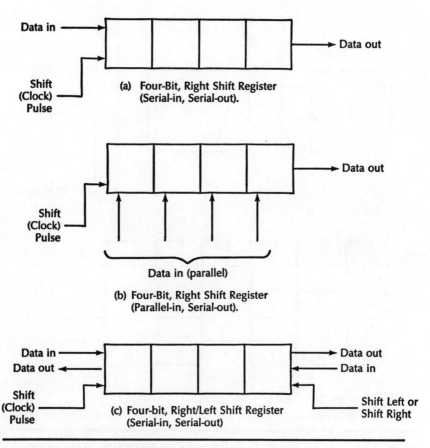

Figure 2.12 Three Different Types of Shift Register

that are equivalent to decimal numbers 0 through 3 upon application of count pulses. Counters can be made to count from 0 through 9 (decimal counters) in binary form, or to any desired number before recycling to 0. Counters can count up as just discussed; they can also count down. The patterns produced by the counters can be used as addresses in microcomputer memory or as triggers to initiate certain control actions in the microprocessor.

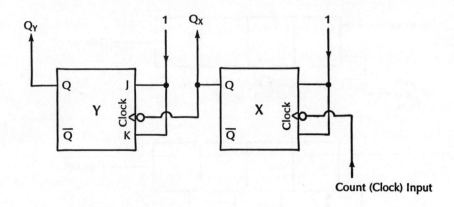

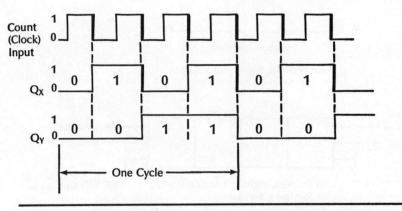

Figure 2.13 Two-Bit Binary Counter and Corresponding Waveforms

2.5 • MICROPROCESSOR IMPLEMENTATION UTILIZING FUNDAMENTAL BUILDING BLOCKS

The combinational and sequential circuits that have just been discussed are the basic building blocks of the microprocessor. The breakthrough that made the microprocessor possible was the discovery of a way to integrate a number of these building blocks onto a single silicon chip. The structure in Figure 2.14 illustrates

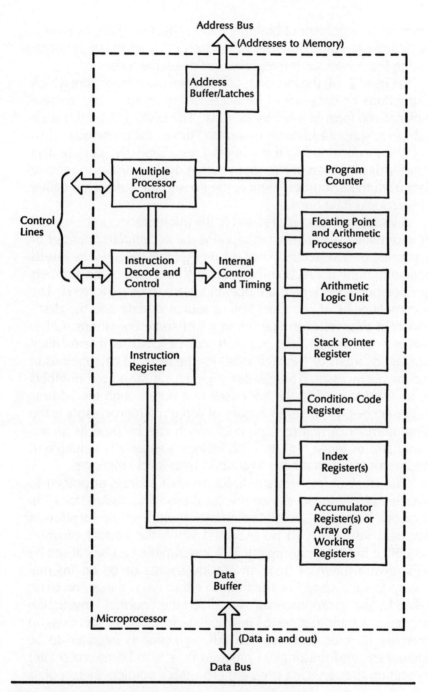

Figure 2.14 Typical Microprocessor Building Blocks

a typical arrangement of building blocks. Bear in mind, however, that there are many different variations of this arrangement composing the numerous microprocessors available today.

In Figure 2.14, the locations or addresses in memory from which instructions or data are to be accessed are held in the address buffer in the form of a binary number. The *buffer* allows the latch outputs to supply additional current to "drive" the numerous memory chips connected to the address lines. Similarly, data buffers transfer data to memory or input/output devices and also receive data from these sources. Hence, the lines to the buffers are called *bidirectional* data lines.

A variety of registers are used in the microprocessor for storage of information. Of particular import is the *accumulator register* or *accumulator*. The accumulator is a register that receives the results of operations in the ALU and also usually holds one of the numbers or *operands* upon which the operations are to be performed. The accumulator or AC is, thus, both a source of data and the destination of data following performance of some operations. Other registers known as *index registers* can be used as intermediate storage locations or "scratchpads" for the result of calculations in the microprocessor. These index registers can also hold numbers to be used to modify the addresses sent out through the address buffer/latches. A powerful feature of some microprocessors is the large number of registers, each of which can be used as an accumulator or index register. This feature is especially valuable in microprocessors that have to support high-level languages.

The *stack pointer register* holds another address or pointer to a series of consecutive memory locations. This "stack area" in memory is used to save intermediate results and the location of the next instruction to be executed when the normal program sequence must be interrupted. This interruption can be caused by a hardware *interrupt* from an outside source or by an internal "jump-to-subroutine" instruction. In either case, the action to be taken by the microprocessor is to divert the "normal" instruction sequence to another set of instructions in different locations in memory. It must be noted that this digression is intended to be temporary, and the original program flow is to be resumed after executing the servicing program. The stack pointer, then, points to a location in memory in which addresses and intermediate data are retained during the digression and then returned after completion of the service program.

The condition code register is made up of flip-flops, each of which indicates a specific condition or status following an instruction execution. Typical conditions include the result negative (sign bit = 1), positive (sign bit = 0), equal to zero, non-zero, a carry generated, or the occurrence of an overflow (result too large for register to hold). By utilizing the set of instructions that checks specific condition code bits, the programmer can provide for alternative choices of action in a program as a function of particular condition codes.

The actual arithmetic and logic operations such as addition, subtraction, shifting, ANDing, and so on are performed in the ALU (Arithmetic Logic Unit). Processors with enhanced arithmetic capability utilize additional floating point hardware or internally contained programs to perform floating point functions. *Floating point* refers to numbers that can be represented in formats not requiring fixed decimal point locations. Examples of floating point numbers are 2.01×10^{-3}, 33.1×10^{6}, 96, 56.103 and .01. *Fixed point* numbers require that the decimal point position remain fixed as in 5.55, 32.01, 56.03, 99.12, and so on. Floating point arithmetic capability usually implies multiplication and division. Advanced microprocessors may also provide some trigonometric, square, and square-root computational functions.

When an instruction is fetched from memory through the bidirectional data bus, it is held in the instruction register for decoding. This decoding examines the *operation code* (binary pattern that specifies the operation to be performed) of the instruction and any operands in the instruction to determine what operations (addition, subtraction, complementing, and so on) are to be carried out. The decoding section working with the control section generates control and timing signals throughout the microprocessor to implement execution of the instruction.

The Program Counter or PC is a counter whose output is used to address the instructions in memory. The counter is incremented after each instruction fetch so that it points to the next location in memory. When an instruction or an external interrupt requires that this sequential flow be changed, the PC must be loaded with the beginning address of the new program to be executed. If it is desired to return to the original program sequence after executing the other program, the old value of the PC must be saved and reloaded into the PC upon completion of the other program. The value of the PC is saved in the memory location specified by the stack pointer.

Some advanced microprocessors have both internal hardware and software to support systems of multiple microprocessors. If common *buses* (connecting paths of wires) are used by these multiple microprocessors, arbitration and bus management techniques are required to avoid conflicts and timing delays among the multiple users of the bus.

In summary, the microprocessor is composed of basic digital blocks that have been integrated on a single silicon chip. This integration makes possible the high concentration of computational power in a minute, low-cost device.

Bibliography

Bartee, T. C. *Digital Computer Fundamentals*. New York: McGraw-Hill, Inc., 1974.

Chu, Y. *Digital Computer Design Fundamentals*. New York: McGraw-Hill, Inc., 1962.

Chapter Three

STORAGE MEDIA

The driving force behind microprocessors, in both a technical and marketing sense, is the semiconductor memory. The memory technology that made the shrinking of components possible was a natural precursor to the microprocessor. Today, because microprocessors require memory devices for operation, the sale of memories and the sale of microprocessors are interdependent.

This chapter will introduce semiconductor technology and discuss specific types of semiconductor memory devices. The related area of disk storage will also be covered at the end of the chapter.

3.1 • INTRODUCTION TO SEMICONDUCTOR TECHNOLOGY

The Metal Oxide Semiconductor (MOS) and bipolar semiconductor technologies were mentioned briefly in section 1.2 of Chapter 1. Recall that the bipolar technology was the first to become commercially developed and widely used in digital circuits.

3.1.1 • Bipolar and MOS Transistors

The bipolar transistor and the logic circuits that were constructed using these transistors were early links in the chain leading to the high-density integrated circuit chips of today. *Bipolar* refers to a transistor in which conduction is composed of both positive and negative charges, hence the term *bipolar conduction*. A modification of the bipolar transistor with a so-called Schottky diode results in a *Schottky bipolar transistor*. Integrated circuits constructed with Schottky bipolar transistors have relatively high speeds of operation, but consume more power and thus cannot be packed as densely as lower power transistors. In the mid-1960's, the MOS or Metal-Oxide-Semiconductor transistor began to gain popularity and became a focal point for the development of high-density, lower power integrated circuits. The MOS transistor is simpler in design than the bipolar transistor and consumes less power. These features of MOS made possible the construction of high-density semiconductor memories and microprocessors.

Both bipolar and MOS transistors are constructed in silicon that is "doped" with (infused with specific amounts and types of) impurities to form regions with an excess of negative or positive charges. The negative silicon areas are called n material and the positive silicon areas are called p material.

The geometry of the n- and p-type areas in the silicon leads to two basic types of bipolar and MOS transistors. There are npn and pnp bipolar transistors and n-channel (NMOS) or p-channel (PMOS) MOS transistors. The structures of each of these devices are given in Figure 3.1.

The name, MOS, was derived from the metal-oxide semiconductor layering in the MOS structure, as shown in Figure 3.2 (see p. 46).

3.1.2 • NMOS and PMOS Transistors

The volume between the two "wells" of either p- or n-type material in the MOS structure is known as the *channel*. The current flow in the MOS transistor is between the *source* (s) region and the *drain* (d) region and is controlled by a voltage on the *gate* (g). When current flows in a MOS transistor, the channel volume near the surface accumulates charge carriers of the type contained in the "wells," and thus, a continuum of the same type of carriers exists in the channel between the wells. The n-channel transistor in conduction in Figure 3.3 (see p. 46) illustrates this operation.

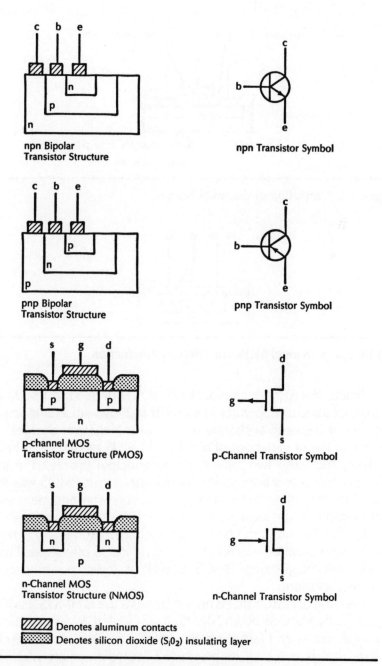

Figure 3.1 Bipolar and MOS Transistor Structures and Symbols

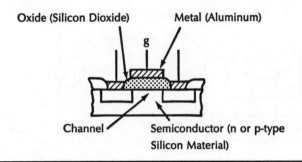

Oxide (Silicon Dioxide)   Metal (Aluminum)

Channel   Semiconductor (n or p-type
Silicon Material)

Figure 3.2 Derivation of the MOS Name

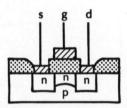

Figure 3.3 n-channel MOS Transistor in Conduction

Hence, the name n channel or NMOS is derived. A PMOS or p-channel transistor operates in a similar fashion with a conducting channel of p (positive) charges instead of n (negative) charges.

A number of variations of bipolar and MOS technologies have evolved, but these two remain as the principal processes in the microprocessor and semiconductor memory areas. PMOS was the first MOS technology to be used in microprocessors and memories and dominated the field from the mid 1960's to approximately 1973. After this time, the NMOS technology matured and is now the dominant semiconductor technology. NMOS offers speed and density advantages over PMOS as well as lower power supply voltage operation.

A version of NMOS that is now in popular use is HMOS. HMOS is essentially a scaled-down NMOS. It was scaled down to achieve higher densities and faster speeds. Another version of MOS technology that is reaching its potential is complementary MOS or CMOS. In CMOS, both n-channel and p-channel transistors are interconnected in a complementary fashion to produce low-power operation. CMOS integrated circuits were introduced by RCA in the 1960's. Their use is now considered a very promising approach to high-density memory and microprocessor circuits because of their low power consumption.

3.2 • SEMICONDUCTOR MEMORIES

The semiconductor memory has led the way for and provided most of the technological basis for the wide variety of digital integrated circuits pervading the commercial, industrial, and consumer markets. Because of the multiple needs of memory users, different types of memories have emerged. In this section, the basic semiconductor memory types will be discussed from a functional point of view. The differences in application and effects on cost and performance will be emphasized. Keep in mind that groups of 1's and 0's are stored in the memories to represent data and instructions to the microprocessor. These 1's and 0's may be stored as open or closed links between two conductors, charge or lack of charge on a capacitor, or conduction or lack of conduction in a transistor.

3.2.1 • ROMs, PROMs, EPROMs, EAROMs, and EEPROMs

This class of semiconductor memories has the characteristic of being *non-volatile*, meaning that the memory contents are not lost when power is removed. This nonvolatility can be achieved in a number of ways. In addition, there are varying degrees of difficulty in writing and rewriting data into these devices. In general, these memories are intended to be primarily *read only*, as opposed to a "scratchpad" or read/write memory. In this discussion, we will proceed toward decreasing difficulty in altering the contents of the memory.

A ROM or Read Only Memory denotes a semiconductor memory whose contents are determined in the final stages of chip fabrication at the factory. The package is then sealed and the contents cannot be altered. Both MOS and bipolar technologies are used in ROM manufacturing. A ROM is used for medium-to-high volume applications where the program stored in the ROM is completely debugged, operates correctly, and will not be changed in the near future. The advantages of using a ROM are its low cost in volume (after paying an initial "masking" charge to customize the information storage patterns) and its reliability. Single-chip ROMs have now reached a storage capacity of 128 kilobits (128 thousand bits). *Access time* or the time interval between presentation of an address to memory and the availability of valid data on the memory output is typically 50 nanoseconds for a bipolar ROM.

The PROM or Programmable Read Only Memory is also unalterable after initial programming but can be programmed by the user at his or her site. The PROM is programmed by "blowing" fusible links at specified addresses inside the memory chip. These links are usually composed of nichrome, polysilicon, titanium-tungsten, and, in some cases, platinum silicide. Single-chip PROM densities range up to 65 kilobits manufactured in Schottky bipolar technology with access times ranging from 40 to 90 ns. Another, less widely used technology for fusible link PROMs is CMOS or complementary MOS.

The EPROM or Erasable Programmable Read Only Memory has the feature of user programmability with reusability. The EPROM was introduced by Intel Corporation circa 1972 and is based on an MOS transistor structure that retains information by means of stored charges in an insulated "floating" gate portion of the MOS transistor. This programming must be done outside the circuit in which the EPROM will operate and is accomplished electrically. Erasure of the EPROM is performed by shining high-intensity ultraviolet light through a quartz window in the EPROM package onto the silicon chip. The energy provided by the UV light discharges the trapped charges and bulk erases the complete chip. The EPROM can be reprogrammed following erasure and used over and over again. Note that the EPROM must be programmed and erased outside of the circuit, requiring physical removal of the chip from the socket. EPROMs are available only in PMOS, NMOS, and

CMOS technologies. The highest density EPROMs now available are 64-kilobit NMOS memories. EPROMs are useful in prototyping microprocessor systems and in small volume applications where changes may be required in the program at infrequent intervals. EPROMs have access times in the 250 nanosecond to 1 microsecond range.

In an effort to provide *in situ* modification of memory data while retaining the nonvolatility of the ROM, PROM, and EPROM, the EEPROM was introduced between 1979 and 1980. The EEPROM or Electrically Erasable Programmable Read Only Memory permits in-socket electrical erasure and rewriting of data on a byte (8 bits) basis. Since EPROMs and EEPROMs are usually organized in arrays of eight-bit words or bytes, reading or writing involves eight bits at one time. In 1981, Intel Corporation introduced the 2816 16K bit EEPROM, which is organized as 2K 8 bit words. NMOS technology is used in the fabrication of this device and a mechanism called Fowler-Nordheim tunneling is used to erase and write data. Access time is approximately 300 nanoseconds (300×10^{-9} seconds) for the 2816. The time to erase and rewrite a byte of data into the 2816 is around 20 milliseconds (20×10^{-3} seconds).

The last major type of nonvolatile semiconductor memory is the EAROM or Electrically Alterable Read Only Memory. The operation of the EAROM is similar to that of the EEPROM, except that EAROMs are fabricated with a modification of PMOS technology, MNOS (Metal Nitride Oxide Semiconductor). MNOS was introduced by NCR in the early 1970's, but suffered from manufacturing problems. These problems now seem to have been solved; and in addition to NCR, companies such as General Instrument, Westinghouse, Hitachi, and Nitron are proponents of the MNOS EAROM approach to read/write nonvolatile semiconductor memory. MNOS EAROMs typically are relatively slow with an access time of 0.09 to 5 microseconds (5×10^{-6} seconds). Hitachi has recently introduced an MNOS EAROM with a 350 nanosecond access time and a chip bulk erase time on the order of several milliseconds.

Figure 3.4 summarizes the nonvolatile semiconductor memory family structure and the associated fabrication technologies.

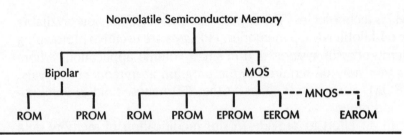

Figure 3.4 Nonvolatile Semiconductor Memory Family Structure

3.2.2 • Read/Write Memory

The semiconductor memory type that revolutionized the semiconductor and computer industry is the read/write memory, or random access memory (RAM) as it is sometimes called. The term RAM means that any location in the memory can be accessed in approximately the same amount of time. The term RAM as applied to read/write memory is somewhat of a misnomer since ROMs, PROMs, EPROMs, EEPROMs, and EAROMs are, in general, random access devices. Read/write memories are volatile and usually have very short access times. These memories are used in large computer systems and minicomputers, as well as microcomputers. RAMs serve as rapid access storage of data and programs; but being volatile, they are subject to loss of data in the event of a power failure unless they are backed up by batteries.

There are two methods of data storage in a RAM: flip-flop storage and storage of charge on MOS capacitors that are part of the circuit on a memory chip. In the capacitor storage method, each bit of information is stored in a memory cell consisting of one or more MOS transistors and a capacitor or capacitors for storage. Since the stored charge representing a 1 or 0 can leak off in a relatively short period of time (approximately 2 milliseconds), the memory cell must be *refreshed* by restoring the charge on the capacitor.

By design, this restoring can be accomplished by reading the memory location or locations to be refreshed at least once every 2 milliseconds. A digital circuit known as a *refresh controller* is used to insure the refreshing of all memory locations every 2 milliseconds—interleaved with the conventional memory accesses in-itiated by the microcomputer in its normal program execution. A read/write memory requiring the refreshing previously described is known as a *dynamic RAM* memory. A read/write memory that doesn't require refreshing is defined as a *static* RAM. In general, static RAMs have lower access times than dynamic RAMs (100–200 ns), are easier to use since they don't require refresh circuits, and are less subject to electrical interference. Dynamic RAMs in general are denser than static RAMs, are cheaper than static RAMs, and require less standby or backup power. Advances in fabrication capabilities are bringing dynamic and static RAM characteristics closer together. Dynamic NMOS RAM densities are presently at the 64K bit level with 256K bit devices expected in the next few years. Experimental NMOS dynamic RAMs with 512K bit and 1M bit (megabit—10^6 bits) densities have been developed experimentally (not in a production environment) by the Japanese Cooperative VLSI Research Laboratory in one of its final programs. Static NMOS RAM densities range to 16K bits with 32K bit and 64K bit versions soon to follow. Access times of the 16K bit static RAMs introduced by Motorola, Intel, and Mostek are from 45 to 55 nanoseconds, rivaling the usually faster but less dense, bipolar, static RAMs. With the improvements in NMOS static RAMs, CMOS static RAMs are making rapid advances in the areas of cost, speed, and density and may one day challenge the NMOS static RAM technology.

3.2.3 • NOVRAM

A device has been introduced by Xicor and General Instruments that provides the high in-circuit read/write speed of a RAM with the nonvolatility of a ROM. This memory chip is called a NOVRAM for Nonvolatile (Static) RAM. The Xicor X2201 and the GI ER1711 combine both RAM and EEPROM on a single silicon chip. The RAM portion of the device operates in the normal high speed read/write fashion and, on command, copies a snapshot of its contents into the backup EEPROM. Similarly, in a restore operation, the EEPROM can update the volatile RAM in the event of loss of data due to a power failure.

3.2.4 • Memory Organization

Semiconductor memories can be internally organized in a variety of ways. A byte-oriented memory, for example, outputs eight bits for every location addressed. The 2K by 8 bit (16K bit) memory as shown in Figure 3.5 illustrates this byte orientation.

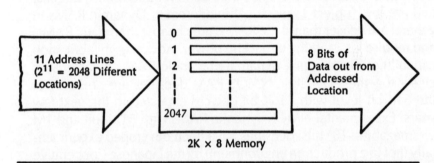

2K × 8 Memory

Figure 3.5 2K by 8 Bit Memory

Note that in specifying memory densities such as 2K, 4K, and 16K, the densities are really the powers of 2: 2,048, 4,096, and 16,384. Memory chips that are organized on a bit basis can be used to implement a variety of memory sizes. For example, 4, 1K × 1 bit memories can implement a 1K × 4 bit memory as in Figure 3.6. Memory chips also have enable or select pins that can disable the memory data out lines and essentially disconnect them from any external circuit. Outputs of this type are termed *tri-state* since they can have a value of 0, 1, or disconnected. The disconnected mode is usually referred to as the *high impedance state* since it presents no loading to the external circuit. Tri-state capability in a memory permits the outputs of a number of memory chips to be attached to common wires without interfering with each other. This sharing of a common memory bus is accomplished by disabling (putting in tri-state mode) memory outputs from all chips except one. The enabled memory chip provides the data out. The enable line is usually derived from the address bits sent out by the microprocessor. An example of tri-state memory operation with two memory chips is given in Figure 3.7. The eleventh address line (A_{10}) selects

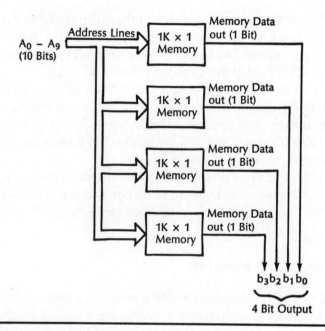

Figure 3.6 1K by 4 Bit Memory

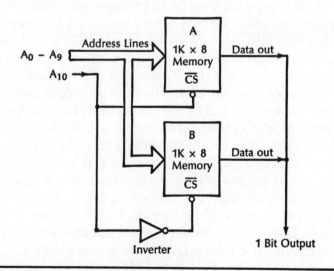

Figure 3.7 Tri-State Memory Operation

one of the memories and disables the other. The circle on the chip select (CS) input of the memory chip indicates that the chip is enabled by an *active low* (a logic 0) on the select pin. A bar over the letters CS ($\overline{\text{CS}}$) also indicates an active low input.

The inverter in the chip select line for memory B insures that only one of the two memory chips is enabled at any one time. For example, a logic 0 placed on address line A will select memory A (active low CS input), but will not select chip B since the inverter will place a 1 (inverted 0) on CS of B.

The chip select line provided by the memory chips can be used to expand memory sizes by word length (number of bits in a word) and by the number of words in the memory array.

3.2.5. • CCD Memory

CCD or Charge Coupled Device memory is a shift-register type of device that circulates packets of charge representing 1's and 0's. By continually recirculating these charge packets, the CCD acts as a memory whose 1's and 0's can be tapped as they rotate by. Since CCD fabrication is based on MOS technology and is conducive to high-density packing, CCD memories were once thought to be the best candidates for high-density semiconductor memories (64K bits, 256K bits). The disadvantage of CCDs is their serial organization resulting in average access time to first bit (sometimes known as *latency time*) of 410 microseconds. The character, then, of CCD memories, seemed to lend them to disk replacement devices. Unfortunately for CCDs, the money and effort put into the development of NMOS technology have made available 64K bit RAMs with random access capability and access times of 50 nanoseconds or less. With a RAM of this type available at comparable cost, why would anyone want a serial access, shift-register type CCD that is orders of magnitude slower? Of course, because most people don't want a slower device, the CCD is in low demand and most CCD manufacturers are phasing out their efforts in this area—except for some selected applications. For example, CCDs that are fabricated to be sensitive to light are finding use in solid state TV cameras and other imaging systems.

3.2.6. • Magnetic Bubble Memory

Magnetic bubble memory is also seen as a challenger to magnetic disk technology; but, unlike CCD memory, it seems destined to successfully invade the three-billion-dollar disk market. Although magnetic bubble technology has only a 30-million- to 35-million-dollar share of the disk market at the present time, bubbles are expected to be highly competitive with disks by 1985 or 1986. Since magnetic bubble memories are fabricated using semiconductor technology and have no moving parts, they are more rugged than disk memories, which involve mechanical rotation of the disks and magnetic heads to store and retrieve data as the disks rotate.

The magnetic bubble memory was invented by Andrew Bobeck of Bell Laboratories in the 1960s. The bubble phenomenon occurs when an external magnetic field is applied to a thin film of ferromagnetic single crystal material (material whose crystals are of uniform orientation). This external field causes magnetic domains or "bubbles" to form which are normal to the film surface. The presence of a bubble in the film represents a stored 1 and the absence of a bubble indicates a stored 0. The bubbles can be caused to move in a shift-register fashion upon the application of a rotating magnetic field to the film. Bubbles can also be destroyed or erased by the proper application of an intense magnetic field. Since bubbles existing in the field are magnetic in nature, they are not destroyed if power to the memory is removed. Thus, bubble memories are nonvolatile, serial-access (shift register) storage devices. The material that is used commercially as the thin film in which the bubbles are created and propagated is *gadolinium-gallium-garnet* or GGG. The GGG film is grown on a ferromagnetic substrate. The path of bubble propagation is determined by a *permalloy* (20% Fe, 80% Ni) pattern deposited on the chip. The externally applied rotating magnetic field magnetizes the permalloy patterns which set up the magnetic polarities that move the bubbles in shift-register fashion. Asymmetric chevron permalloy patterns are used in a number of commercial products while contiguous disk patterns are being used by Bell Laboratories and IBM in improved experimental devices. Bubble memory chips ranging in density from 64K bits to 1 Mbit were available from such manufacturers as Intel, Rockwell, Texas Instruments, and National Semiconductor. In somewhat surprising moves, Rockwell, Texas Instruments, and National Semiconductor have withdrawn from the commercial bubble memory market because of disappointing demand projections for such a product. Average access or latency time for typical bubble chips are in the 4 to 40 millisecond range with maximum shifting rates of approximately 50KHz to 100KHz. Construction of a typical, packaged magnetic bubble memory chip is given in Figure 3.8.

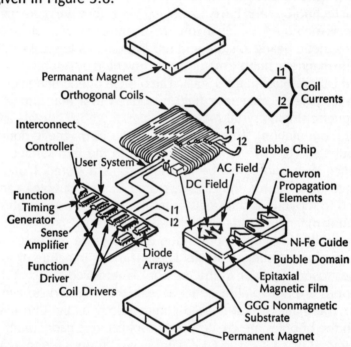

Figure 3.8 Magnetic Bubble Memory Construction

3.2.7. • Summary of Semiconductor Memories and Characteristics

Table 3.1 provides a summary of the important characteristics of the types of semiconductor memories discussed in this chapter. Numbers given are average figures and will naturally change with improvements in technology.

Table 3.1 Summary of Semiconductor Memories

	Random Access/ Access Time	Serial Access/ Access Time	Volatile	Technology	Density	Characteristics
ROM	Yes/50ns	No/NA	No	Schottky bipolar MOS, CMOS	up to 128K	For large volume, final designs. Custom masking, fast.
PROM	Yes/50ns	No/NA	No	Schottky bipolar CMOS	up to 64K	Lower volume, in-house programming, fast.
EPROM	Yes/250ns–1us	No/NA	No	MOS, CMOS	up to 64K	Out of socket erasure and programming, prototyping.
EEPROM	Yes/250ns–500ns	No/NA	No	MOS	up to 16K	Write time of 20 ms, byte erase.
EAROM	Yes/350ns–5us	No/NA	No	MNOS	up to 16K	Byte erase.
RAM	Yes/45ns–450ns	No/NA	Yes	NMOS	up to 128K	High-speed, high-density, read/write.
NOVRAM	Yes/250ns	No/NA	No	MOS, MNOS	1K static RAM, 1K EEPROM	Volatile RAM backed up by "shadow" EEPROM.
CCD	No/NA	Yes/410 usec	Yes	MOS	up to 256K	Shift register type memory. May disappear from high volume marketplace because of MOS RAM advances.
BUBBLE	No/NA	Yes/20 ms	No	GGG or ferromagnetic substrate	up to 1M	Disk replacement. Higher densities will appear.

3.3. • DISK STORAGE FOR MICROPROCESSORS

Storage of large amounts of data and programs that can be loaded into RAM for execution and analysis is usually accomplished in disk storage. The magnetic disk is similar in appearance to a phonograph record and stores the information as magnetically written 1's and 0's. The unit containing the mechanical rotating and read/write equipment to place information on the disk and extract information from the disk is called a *disk drive*. Two popular versions are *flexible* or *floppy disk* and a *Winchester disk*. A typical floppy disk that stores data on both sides at double density holds approximately 1.6 Mbytes of data while the average Winchester holds approximately 20 Mbytes. Average access time for a double-sided/double-density floppy disk is on the order of 100 to 300 milliseconds while an average Winchester disk access time is on the order of 30 to 170 milliseconds. For reliability, the Winchester drives are completely sealed for the protection of the disk and read/write mechanism. Floppy disks are not sealed and are subject to contamination from cigarette smoke, fingerprints, and dust particles. Such contamination manifests itself in error rates for read/write accesses to the disk.

Winchester drives come in 5¼-inch (micro-Winchester), 8-inch, and 14-inch sizes, with the 5¼- and 8-inch drives used for microcomputer applications. Table 3.2 summarizes the salient features of Winchester and flexible disk technology for microprocessor applications.

The Shugart Associates SA 1000 8-inch Winchester disk drive is shown in Figure 3.9 (see p. 60).

Table 3.2 Summary of Winchester and Flexible Disk Technology

	Average Access Time	Capacity (Mbytes)	Data Rate (Mbits/sec)	Physical Size (in.)	Device Cost
Flexible	100–300ms	1.6	0.5	4.62 × 8.55 × 14.25	$400–$600
8" Winchester	30–70ms	5–30	4.5	4.62 × 8.55 × 14.25	$1,000–$2,000
5¼" Winchester	170ms	6.38	5	5¾ × 3¼ × 8	$925

Figure 3.9 View of Shugart SA 1000 8″ Winchester Disk Drive

3.4. • COMPARISON OF MEMORY ALTERNATIVES

To conclude this chapter, Figures 3.10 and 3.11 are presented to put the various memory alternatives in perspective in relation to speed of access, cost, and storage capacity. Disk storage offers low cost per bit and high density at the expense of access time. At the other end of the spectrum, semiconductor memory offers rapid access, lower density than disks, but a relatively high cost per bit. CCD and magentic bubble memories are so called "gap-filler" technologies, bridging the gap between semiconductor memories and disk storage.

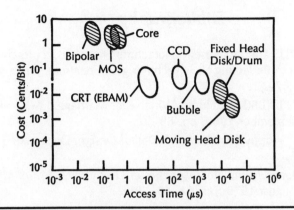

Figure 3.10 Memory Cost per Bit versus Access Time

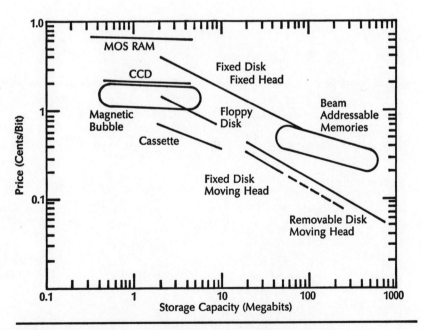

Figure 3.11 Memory Cost per Bit versus Storage Capacity

Bibliography

Bernhard, R. "US and Japanese Manufacturers Reached Impressive Milestones in Perfecting VLSI Technology." *Spectrum,* January 1981, pp. 57–61.

Deemer, K. "DSD 880—A Floppy/Winchester Marriage." *Mini-Micro Systems,* September 1980, pp. 89–92.

Goodman, G. "Floppy Disk Drives." *Digital Design,* December 1979, pp. 62–66.

Trifai, J. "Backing Up the New Winchester Disk Drives." *Mini-Micro Systems,* August 1979, pp. 44–48.

Chapter Four

MICROPROCESSORS/ MICROCOMPUTERS

4.1 • MICROPROCESSOR ARCHITECTURAL CONSIDERATIONS

A microcomputer is comprised of a microprocessor or CPU (central processing unit), program memory, data memory, input/output circuits, and timing (clock) circuits. The microprocessor itself consists of an arithmetic logic unit (ALU) and associated internal storage and control circuitry. The organization of the digital building blocks in the microprocessor and the information paths among those blocks is referred to as the microprocessor *architecture*.

A microprocessor can also be viewed in terms of its *instruction set,* or the list of instructions it is designed to execute. Evaluations among microprocessors, or in fact any processor, can be made by comparing the memory usage efficiencies and the speeds of programs executed using the instructions given on the various microprocessors. A processor described in terms of its instruction set is said to have a particular *instruction set architecture.* This description is independent of the detailed technology with which the processor is built and depends solely on characteristics of the processor that are stated in its set of instructions.

A third definition of microprocessor architecture is used by the system designer, who views it as the integration of computer hardware and software into a system designed to perform a specific set of functions. This view of architecture can be termed *system architecture*.

4.1.1 • General Architectural Considerations

In order to meet the needs of the executive/manager who is the reader of this book, architectural considerations among all three areas will be discussed. Each reader will then be able to discern his or her own appropriate definition of architecture.

Because the building blocks of the microprocessor include components such as the ALU, storage registers, program counter (PC), stack pointer register (SP), condition code register, instruction decoder, and accumulator register(s), there exist numerous alternatives to their employment and interconnection. The motivation behind the different architectures resulting from these alternatives is usually a function of the intended product market and application. For example, an architecture may be intended to support the execution of a particular high-level language, multi-microcomputer applications, or industrial process control. Some architectural features are historical, wherein a newly introduced processor retains some features of an earlier product to maintain upward software compatibility between both products. The progression of the Intel microprocessors beginning with the eight-bit 8008 to the eight-bit 8080 up to the eight-bit 8085 is a good example of upward software compatibility affecting new product architectures. Even the 16-bit 8086 processor from Intel carries architectural traces back to the 8008–8085 progression.

4.2 • ARCHITECTURAL EXAMPLES

In order to better understand microprocessor architectures and some of the factors behind them, let's examine some real architectures from a functional point of view. The architectures chosen are those of the MOS Technology 6502, the Intel 432 micromainframe, the Motorola 68000, and the Zilog Z8000. The 6502 was chosen because it is a good example of a well-designed eight-bit architecture. The others chosen represent today's leading micro-processors and incorporate architectural features that will prolif-erate in the decade of the 1980's.

4.2.1 • The MOS Technology 6502

The architecture of the 6502 microprocessor is given in Figure 4.1 on the next page.

Note that to the left of the figure, there is a 16-bit address bus that is used to specify data and instruction locations in memory. The 16 lines present patterns of 1's and 0's to the memories with 2^{16}, or 65,536, of these patterns possible. In contrast to the address bus which is unidirectional, the data bus at the bottom of the figure is bidirectional, meaning that binary information can pass into or out of the microprocessor on these lines. The bidirectional lines permit data transfer in one direction at a time. The ready (RDY) input line at the right of the figure permits a slow memory (usually an EPROM) to "freeze" the processor until the memory has enough time to present the requested data to the microprocessor on the data bus. For the 1 MHz version of the 6502 microprocessor, memories with access times greater than 500 nanoseconds must use the ready line since the processor assumes correct information is present on the data bus after an access time of 500 nanoseconds maximum. If valid data are not available, the microprocessor will read "garbage" on the data bus. The reset ($\overline{RES}$), interrupt request ($\overline{IRQ}$), and nonmaskable interrupt ($\overline{NMI}$) lines at the top of the figure have the ability to force the microprocessor to start executing a program at fixed, previously defined locations. The reset line, when activated (low), causes the microprocessor to start executing a program at a reserved location in nonvolatile memory. The pro-gram beginning at this location performs an initialization sequence, such as that required after power is first applied. Initialization steps may include defining input/output lines and operations, setting particular values on output lines to critical external devices, load-ing certain registers with starting values, and beginning execution of the main program. The $\overline{IRQ}$ and $\overline{NMI}$ interrupt inputs operate

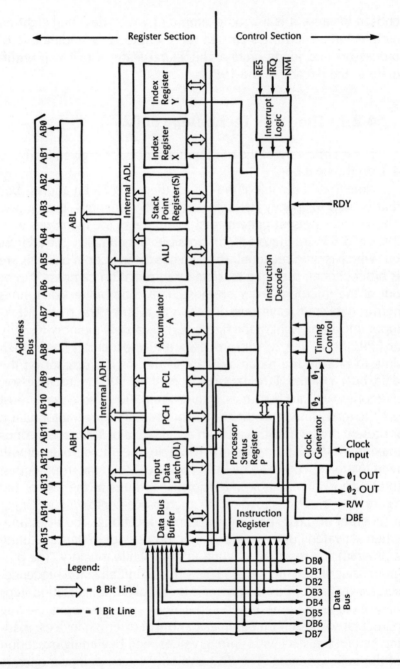

Figure 4.1 Architecture of the 6502 Microprocessor

in an identical manner, except that they each cause program transfer to a different location in memory where other programs can begin execution. These two inputs can be activated by external devices such as a keyboard, alarm indicator, and push button. Activation of $\overline{IRQ}$ and $\overline{NMI}$ by these external devices is a request for service by these devices. The program control then transfers or "vectors" to the predefined location and begins executing the servicing program. After completion of this service routine, the original program sequence continues. $\overline{IRQ}$ and $\overline{NMI}$ each have their own interrupt vector locations. The difference between $\overline{IRQ}$ and $\overline{NMI}$ is that $\overline{IRQ}$ can be disabled and enabled in software by microprocessor instructions whereas the $\overline{NMI}$ cannot. Recall that a bar over a line (such as $\overline{IRQ}$) means that it is activated on a low or 0 input and is termed "active low."

The clock input to the 6502 requires a crystal circuit to provide a timing reference source for the microprocessor. The $R/\overline{W}$ line indicates to memory or input/output devices that either a read (line = 1) or a write (line = 0) is taking place.

Without belaboring the issue, let us briefly look at the architecture (building blocks) of the 6502 as shown in Figure 4.1. The address of the next instruction to be executed is present in the program counter (PC) and is placed on the address bus.

In the 6502, PCH represents the high order 8 bits and PCL represents the low order 8 bits of the 16 bit PC. Memory is accessed at the address sent out on the address bus and the instruction is returned to the microprocessor via the eight-bit data bus. The instruction pattern (1's and 0's) is held in the instruction register and decoded to identify the instruction and the actions to be taken to execute the instruction. The instruction decoder then sends out control signals to the different portions of the microprocessor to cause the instruction to be executed. The control signals can be generated by logic circuits or by a read-only memory whose address inputs are the 1's and 0's of the instruction pattern and whose outputs are the control signals to implement execution of the instruction. Decoding in this way, by means of code in a memory, is called *microcoding*.

The index registers X and Y are used for internal "scratch pad" storage of intermediate results and also for modifying memory addresses held in the program counter. One of the *addressing modes,* as they are called, will add the contents of an index register to the address value held in the program counter, and the resulting sum is then sent out as the memory address. This mode is particularly useful if it is desired to proceed through a table of numbers in consecutive memory locations. By incrementing the value in the index register, the address sent out will increase by one at each memory access. When the incrementing of the index register is done automatically without requiring a specific instruction by the programmer, the microprocessor is said to have an *auto increment* feature.

The remaining building blocks serve the same functions as described earlier in the text. In summary, the accumulator holds results of operations, holds values to be operated upon, and is the register normally used in data transfers involving the microprocessor and memory or input/output devices. The stack pointer is similar to the PC, but points to locations in memory (or stack) where the PC is automatically stored during an interrupt service or a call to a subroutine. After the service routine or subroutine is completed, the value of the PC is automatically restored from the stack and the original program continues execution. Finally, the processor status register provides information following the execution of instructions. The status register provides flip-flops that are set if a negative result occurs; a carry is generated following an operation; an overflow of the capacity of the accumulator occurs; and so on. Those flip-flops or "flags" can cause "branches" of the program to different locations in memory if specific branch instructions are executed. A typical branch instruction may be BRN xxxx which is interpreted as "branch to location xxxx in memory if the status register indicates a negative result." In this way, decisions can be made dynamically by the program as it is being executed.

The 6502 is not a new microprocessor, but is a good representation of the eight-bit devices that emerged around 1974. It is still widely used and is the processor in the popular Apple II and Commodore "Pet" personal computers.

4.2.2 • The Intel iAPX 432

The Intel iAPX 432 is the leading commercially available microprocessor. The 432 is actually a mainframe computer implemented on three silicon chips. The 432 architecture provides 32-bit mainframe functionality, has facilities to support high-level software, and supports addition of multiple processors. The address space that is instantaneously addressable by the 432 is 2^{32} locations with 2^{40} locations addressable through software supported (virtual) accesses.

The iAPX 432 consists of three chips. The iAPX 43201 and iAPX 43202 comprise the 32-bit general data processor (GDP) while the iAPX 43203 is an interface processor. The iAPX 43201 has an impressive density of 100K transistors on the single chip while the 43202 and 43203 each have densities of 60K transistors.

A significant feature of the 432 architecture is that it supports the kernel or heart of the operating system internally. In other words, the major portion of the operating system resides "in silicon" on the 432 chips. The operating system is a program resident, in ROM on the 43201 and 43202 chips, that manages system resources, schedules processes, manages the processor, allocates storage, and provides protected memory spaces.

The 432 micromainframe also supports the Ada high-level language sponsored by the U.S. Department of Defense (DoD). Ada will be discussed in more detail in Chapter 5, but a brief description of its highlights will be presented here to reflect supporting features of the 432 architecture.

Ada can be defined as a language aimed at real-time applications with concurrent execution requirements. Ada is based on the language Pascal (also to be discussed in Chapter 5), but directly supports multiple task execution and communication. Strong data typing, which means that the programmer must define the attributes of his or her data before program execution, ensures that a large number of errors are detectable by the Ada compiler software at the time of program compilation. Detection at this time is desirable since the alternative is detection of errors by unpredictable actions during actual execution of the program or "run time." The 432 architecture also enhances the decomposition of large programs into smaller, manageable modules whose interconnections are separate from their contents. This approach permits multiple programmers to work on complex software development problems and also allows for later modification of program modules without affecting other parts of the program.

The GDP components of the 432, the 43201 and the 43202, operate as *pipelined* units. In a pipeline approach, instruction fetching, decoding, and execution times are overlapped so that a new instruction can be fetched while the present instruction is being executed. This pipelining serves to speed up the throughput of instructions in the processor. In the 432 system, the 43201 instruction decoder unit fetches and decodes the instruction while the 43202 execution unit executes the instruction. The 43203 interface processor provides the address, data, and control interfaces between the GDP and the remaining portions of the computer system.

4.2.3 • The Zilog Z8000

The Zilog Z8000 is a 16-bit microprocessor that provides mini-computer-like capability in a microprocessor. In terms of power and technology, it falls between conventional eight-bit microprocessors, such as the Intel 8085 or Motorola 6800, and the Intel 432 micromainframe. The Z8000 is available in two versions, the Z8001 and the Z8002. The Z8001 is a 48-pin device that can address up to 6 distinct memory areas, each containing 128 segments of 65,536 bits. With this capability, termed *memory segmentation,* the Z8001 can address up to 48M bytes. The Z8002 is identical to the 48-pin Z8001 except that "only" 6 memory spaces of 65,536 bits each can be addressed. A feature of the Z8000 is the normal/system output that can be used to separate memory space into a user area and a system area. With this separation, a user is in the normal mode and cannot gain access to critical parameters that might disrupt the system operation. In other words, users of the system can be kept from modifying critical system parameters, but can work in the normal mode on their own parameters without restriction.

Internally, the Z8000 provides registers for manipulating 8-bit words (bytes), 16-bit words, and 32-bit words (long words). Specifically, the registers available are accessible as sixteen 8-bit registers, sixteen 16-bit registers, eight 32-bit registers, or four 64-bit registers. Because of increased memory addressing capacity of the Z8000, there are some differences in the register structures of the Z8001 and Z8002 microprocessors. The register organization of both devices is given in Figure 4.2 on the next page.

4.2.4 • The Motorola 68000

The Motorola MC68000 is another one of the 16-bit microprocessors that has minicomputer-like features. The 68000 is designed to support high-level languages with specific language-oriented instructions in its instruction set, multiple internal registers, and large addressing range. The address bus of the 68000 is 24 bits, which permits addressing of 16,777,216 bytes of memory.

The 68000 microprocessor provides seventeen 32-bit registers plus a 32-bit program counter and a 16-bit status register as shown in Figure 4.3 on p. 73.

One group of eight 32-bit data registers (registers D0 to D7) can also be accessed as 8-bit registers, 16-bit registers, and 32-bit registers. Address registers A_0 to A_6 and the stack pointer can be used in 16- or 32-bit address operations as well as being used as software stack pointers. As in the Z8000, the system can be in either the user state or supervisory state with corresponding stack pointers and status registers for each state. The user state is a lower state of privilege and prohibits execution of instructions such as stop or halt.

The 68000 provides multiprocessor support through hardware and software interlocks, bus arbitration logic for shared bus and shared memory environment, and instructions to perform testing and setting functions. The programming support features include instructions to reduce the time involved in calling subroutines and instructions that have the same mnemonic for 8-bit, 16-bit, and 32-bit instructions. Some other computers have different mnemonics for the same instruction with different lengths.

The Motorola 68000, as some other 16- and 32-bit micropro-

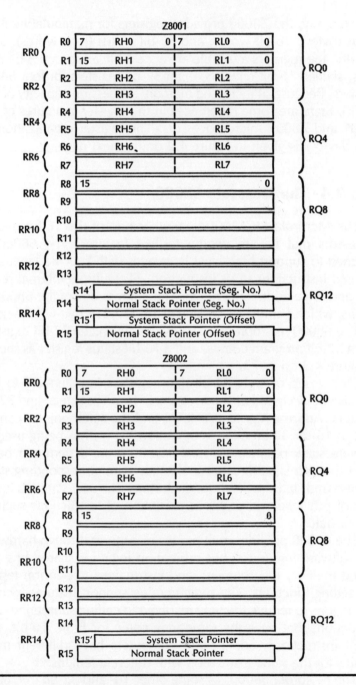

Figure 4.2 Register Organization of the Z8001 and Z8002 Microprocessors

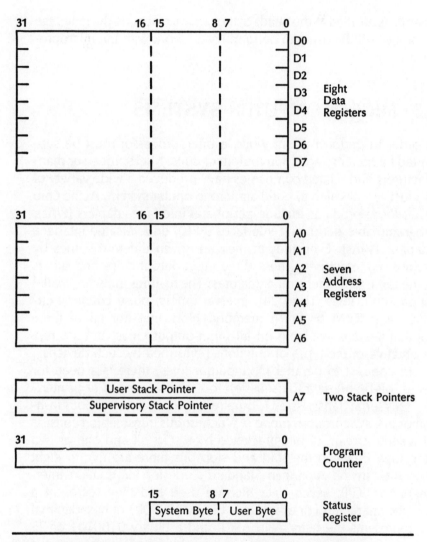

Figure 4.3 Register Organization of the 68000 Microprocessor

cessors, is attuned to the needs of the programmer and the language he or she will be using to perform useful work with the microprocessor.

4.3 • MICROCOMPUTER SYSTEMS

In order to perform useful work, a microprocessor must be supported by memory and input/output circuits. Microprocessor manufacturers and related companies have produced a wide variety of products with which to build a microcomputer system. At the chip level, these products include peripheral interface adapters (PIAs), programmable peripheral interfaces (PPIs), and versatile interface adapters (VIAs). Even though they are given different names by various manufacturers, these three input/output chips and others of the same type offer similar features. The features include parallel input/output lines (16 to 24), interval timers, pulse counting circuits, and RAM or ROM memory. Note that not all of these capabilities are available on all input-output chips, but are representative of the types of functions performed by such devices.

In contrast to parallel input/output lines, there is a need for serial, bit-by-bit data transmission to a video terminal or printer.

This serial transmission is usually sent in an *asynchronous* fashion or in a *synchronous* mode. Asynchronous transmission consists of a serial stream of bits bracketed by a start bit and one or two stop bits. Between the start and stop bits there are five to eight data bits. In the American Standard Code for Information Interchange (ASCII), seven data bits are used and they represent a specific character. For example, a binary 1000001 or hexadecimal 41 represents the letter A in ASCII and a binary 0100101 or 25 hexadecimal represents the % sign. A table of ASCII characters is given in Appendix A. A popular chip for implementing asynchronous transmission and reception with a microcomputer is a universal asynchronous receiver transmitter or UART. When used as a transmitter, the UART accepts data from the data bus of the microprocessor, optionally adds a check bit (*parity* bit), and adds the start and stop bits. The parity bit permits detection by the receiver of a single bit error in transmission. As a receiver, the UART performs the parity check, gives an indication of a parity error (if any), strips the incoming word of the start and stop bits, and presents the data word to the receiving microprocessor's data bus.

Another type of serial transmitter/receiver is the universal synchronous/asynchronous receiver transmitter or USART. With a USART, serial data can be transmitted synchronously at a higher rate than with asynchronous transmission. Instead of using start and stop bits, a clock pulse generator of the same frequency is used at both the transmitter and receiver to respectively generate and sample the transmitted data bits. For this method to work, both clock generators must be synchronized. To accomplish this synchronization, a SYNC character or characters of a known pattern are generated by the transmitting USART and searched for by the receiving USART. When the SYNC character is identified by the receiver, the two clock generators are in synchronism and the data can be properly understood by the receiver. Most USARTs can operate in either the asynchronous or synchronous mode.

Other devices that can be used to construct a microcomputer system are refresh controllers to handle refreshing of dynamic memory, floppy disk controllers to interface the microcomputer to floppy disk drives, and *direct memory access* (DMA) controllers that allow high speed data exchanges between microcomputer memory and external devices such as disk storage. This direct access time is limited essentially by the access time of the memory, in contrast to data transfers through the microprocessor's accumulator(s) that are limited by the execution times of instructions necessary to accomplish the transfer.

Complete systems called *microprocessor development systems* (MDS) are available from microprocessor manufacturers that provide both hardware and software support to the system developer. These systems usually consist of a packaged microcomputer with expandable amounts of RAM and ROM, disk storage, a video terminal, and a hard copy printer. Development systems offered by microcomputer manufacturers provide in-depth support for their particular products, but do not usually support products of other companies. Typical of these systems are the Intel Intellec series and the Motorola EXORciser and EXORmacs. Conversely, some instrument manufacturers such as Hewlett-Packard and Tektronix have produced development systems that support a number of microprocessors from different manufacturers.

The HP 64000 development system can have up to six users at a time performing development work on different microcomputers. Most development systems provide high-level language support such as Pascal as well as assembly language, editing, and debugging software. Development system costs can range from approximately $8,000 to $100,000. A typical development system is shown in Figure 4.4.

Two different development philosophies have emerged that are important to note. One is to perform development on a dedicated system provided by the microprocessor manufacturer and the other is to utilize a general purpose computer, perhaps a minicomputer, to support development of a number of different microprocessors. The latter concept is embodied in the HP 64000 system, but can be carried further to be run on a truly general computer system. This idea was formalized at Bell Laboratories by Evan L. Ivie as the programmer's workbench (PWB) concept. Basically the concept states that software development and final product development environments are different and have contradictory requirements. In software development, the user needs flexibility, sophisticated programming tools, debugging aids, documentation, and maintenance support. The final product needs include small amounts of memory, low cost, high throughput, minimum size, and so on. To meet these contrasting needs, Ivie proposed a programmer's workbench computer system that would give the developer all the tools he or she needed to develop and debug software for a variety of target microprocessors. These tools would include management features, such as tracking of changes, scheduling and report generators, as well as assemblers, high-level language compilers, and simulators for the different target microprocessors. Furthermore, the grammatical rules for using these compilers and assemblers would be standard so that a relearning process would not be required when going from one microprocessor to another. This relearning is required when using development systems from different manufacturers. Figure 4.5 is a pictorial representation of the PWB concepts (see p. 78).

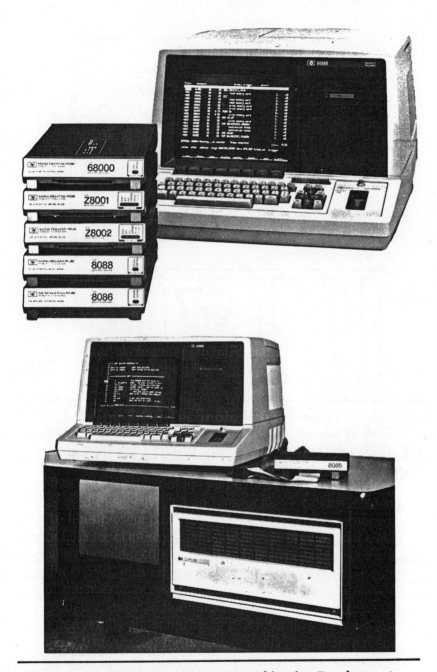

Figure 4.4   Hewlett-Packard HP 64000 Multistation Development System

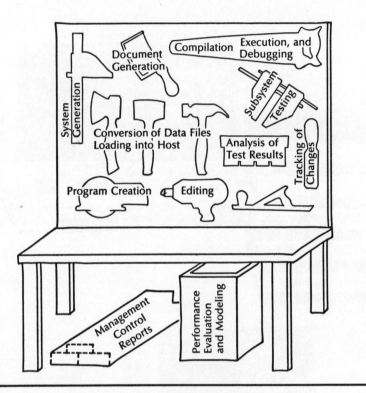

Figure 4.5 Programmer's Workbench Concept

4.4 • INTERFACING CONSIDERATIONS AND STANDARDS

4.4.1 • Interfacing Considerations

Interface refers to a boundary. In a microcomputer system, it refers to the boundary between the microprocessor and the outside world. The outside world could be a disk drive, lights, switches, a printer, or even another microprocessor. A block diagram of a typical interface is given in Figure 4.6.

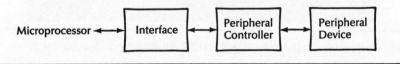

Figure 4.6 Block Diagram of a General Microprocessor Interface

The interface block is selected by the address bus and takes data from the microprocessor data bus. It can provide input/output lines, handle interrupts, and format data. The UART and USART discussed in section 4.3 are interface chips.

The peripheral controller is specific to the peripheral device. For example, if the peripheral controller were a floppy disk controller, it would provide outputs such as headload (causing the read/write head to contact diskette), head select (selecting one of a number of read/write heads), and read/write/seek (commanding the disk drive to either seek a new location on diskette or perform a read or write). A cathode ray tube (CRT) controller chip for use in a video display terminal supplies signals for controlling the horizontal and vertical retraces of the scan lines on the screen, controlling the cursor, and detecting input from an operator with a light pen. A light pen is a hand-held pen-like pointer that can be used to select a specific portion of a display and input data to the controlling computer.

In many instances, the functions of the interface chip and the peripheral controller chip have been combined into a single chip that performs both functions.

A popular type of peripheral chip that is not an interface, but should be noted here is the *arithmetic processing unit*. This device appears as memory to the microprocessor, accepts data written from the microprocessor, and returns processed data to the microprocessor. Typically, the arithmetic chips perform fixed point and floating addition, subtraction, multiplication, and division, trigonometric operations, square roots, logarithms, and exponentiation.

4.4.2 • Standards

In order to ease the burden of interconnecting microcomputer-based systems and external equipment (either local or remote), some standards have been developed. A popular standard for synchronous serial communication is Synchronous Data Link Control (SDLC). SDLC defines a communications protocol for transmission of data from one location to another. Information is sent in an SDLC frame as shown in Figure 4.7.

Open Flag	Address Field (A)	Control Field (C)	Information Field (I)	Frame Check Sequence (FCS)	Close Flag
01111110	8 Bits	8 Bits	Any Length up to N Bits in Multiples of 8 Bits	16 Bits	01111110

Figure 4.7 SDLC Frame Format

SDLC was developed by IBM and has been widely adopted as a communications protocol. Microprocessor manufacturers have made SDLC controller chips available to implement this protocol.

Other widely used serial interface standards are the Electronic Industries Association EIA RS-232-C and the EIA RS-422 and RS-423. These standards specify voltage and current levels, timing, and loading conditions for data transfer among electrical instruments and related equipment. RS-232 is an older specification (1969) while RS-422 and RS-423 are 1975 upgrades of RS-232. These standards also define connector types and pin assignments on the connectors for the various interface signals.

A parallel instrumentation interface standard is the IEEE-488-1978 interface bus. This standard evolved from the Hewlett Packard Instrumentation Bus (HPIB) introduced by HP to permit interconnections among its instrument and computer lines. IEEE-488 is also referred to as the General Purpose Interface Bus or GPIB. The IEEE-488 defines instruments as a talker (sends data), a listener (receives data), and a controller. Instruments can have one or all of these attributes, but there can only be one controller in the system. The IEEE-488 bus is broken into three subgroups: the eight-line data bus, the three-line handshake bus, and the five-line general interface management bus. The IEEE-488 bus structure is shown in Figure 4.8.

The IEEE-488 standard is widely used by a variety of instrument and computer manufacturers and is supported by GPIB chips developed by the semiconductor vendors. These GPIB chips are driven by the microprocessor and provide the proper voltage levels, input/output lines, and timing to implement the IEEE-488 bus.

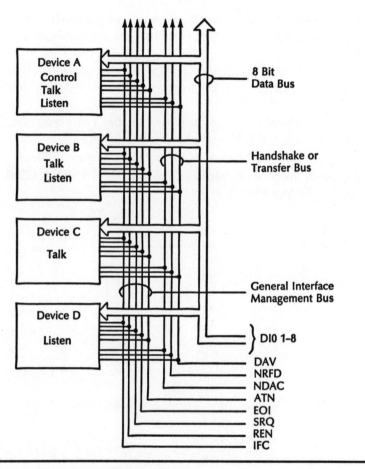

Figure 4.8 IEEE-488 Bus Structure

Bibliography

Bernhard, Robert. "Micros and Software." *Spectrum,* January 1980, pp. 38–41, New York, New York.

Comerford, Richard W. "Development System Networks: The Last Link in Automated Manufacturing." *Electronics,* July 3, 1980, pp. 124–142.

Component Data Catalog. Intel Corporation, 1980.

EIA Standard RS-422: Electrical Characteristics of Balanced Voltage Digital Interface Circuits. Electronic Industries Association, April 1975.

EIA Standard RS-423: Electrical Characteristics of Unbalanced Voltage Digital Interface Circuits. Electronic Industries Association, April 1975.

IEEE Standard Digital Interfaces for Programmable Instrumentation, Standard 488–1978. New York: IEEE Standards.

Peripheral Design Handbook. Intel Corporation, August 1980.

SDLC General Information Manual, GA27–3093–1, File No. GENL–09. IBM Corporation, May 1975.

Chapter Five

MICROCOMPUTER SOFTWARE

Software development is one of the most critical issues a manager must deal with in the area of microcomputers. Because software development is labor intensive, its associated costs are increasing more and more—in contrast to the decreasing hardware costs that have resulted from advances in semiconductor processing technology.

5.1. • DEFINITIONS

As there are numerous categories of software, it may be helpful to define some of the most popular categories. Some of the following definitions have already been given in earlier chapters, but they will be repeated here to complete the discussion.

Beginning with the microcomputer hardware, the 1's and 0's (high voltages and low voltages) that form patterns that can be decoded by the microprocessor make up its *machine language*. Thus, 10001110 may be the machine language representation of the instruction to clear (reset) a register, say register A. The execution of this instruction will cause register A to contain all 0's. Of course, the pattern 10001110 has no inherent meaning to the human user. In order to enhance the understanding and utilization of the microprocessor's instruction, each machine language instruction pattern can be given a name or memory aid that relates to the operation performed by the instruction. For example, the instruction represented by 10001110 to clear register A might have the name or mnemonic CLA that stands for clear register A. Again, note that there is a one-to-one correspondence between the mnemonic CLA and the machine language instruction represented by 10001110.

The collection of mnemonics representing the set of machine instructions is called the *assembly language* of the particular microprocessor. By writing a program to read each mnemonic and then generate the corresponding 1 and 0 pattern, the user can develop his or her applications in assembly language rather than in machine language. The program that performs the one-to-one conversion of assembly language mnemonics to machine language binary patterns is called an *assembler*. Pictorially, this conversion can be represented as in Figure 5.1.

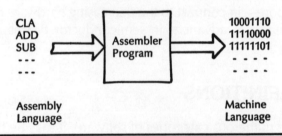

Figure 5.1 Assembly Language to Machine Language Conversion

The assembler program can be run on the microcomputer itself (a *resident assembler*) or on another computer such as a minicomputer *(cross assembler)*.

Assembly language instructions are usually very simple instructions. Typically, they perform additions, subtractions, shifting, resetting, and comparing functions. The more powerful 16- and 32-bit microprocessors can also implement integer and, in some cases, floating point multiplication and division. Atypical of microprocessors in general is the Intel 432 that performs operating system functions and some high-level operations. These features portend the microprocessor developments of the 1980's.

It is obviously desirable to control the microprocessor using higher level instructions. For example, if it was desired to take the square root of a number *n* using the limited set of typical assembly language instructions such as ADD, SUB, SHIFT, etc., a programmer might be able to take the square root of *n* using a clever combination of the available assembly language instructions. Let's say that the square root of *n* can be taken using 15 assembly language instructions. Contrast this method with a high-level language (HLL) or high-order language (HOL) that may have as one of its basic instructions a SQR*(n)* instruction that accomplishes the square root in one statement. High-level languages of this type include FORTRAN, Pascal, Ada, and BASIC. For one of these languages to execute on a particular microprocessor, the high-level statement in that language has to eventually be implemented with the simpler assembly language instructions. This transformation is called *compilation* and is performed by a program called a *compiler*. Thus, a FORTRAN compiler for a Motorola 68000 microprocessor will take a standard FORTRAN high-level statement such as A = B/C and produce a sequence of 68000 assembly language (or machine language) instructions that will effectively perform the high-level operation. Thus, a compiler is machine specific, since it must produce the assembly or machine instructions of a particular machine. However, a program written in a high-level language is, theoretically, transportable among machines that have compilers for the language. This transportability depends heavily on the standardization of the high-level language so that compilers for different microprocessors have the same high-level definitions and instructions to work with. Unfortunately, many manufacturers add "extensions" to a particular high-level language, thus making it nonstandard and unusable by the compiler of a different machine that did not include the handling of these extensions.

Another means of utilizing a high-level language on a microprocessor is through an interpreter. An *interpreter* is a program that takes each high-level language statement in a program and executes it by calling an existing series of machine language instructions. These machine language instructions have been previously developed to perform the required high-level operation and they reside in memory awaiting their selection. Thus, in an interpreter, each high-level program statement must reside in memory as well as in the interpreter programs that execute each of the high-level statements.

Compared to compilers, interpreters execute the high-level statements more slowly and require more memory space, since both the high-level program and the interpreter routines reside in memory at the time of program execution. On the other hand, interpreters are less complex than compilers and easier to implement. BASIC is a popular interpreted language.

Pictorially, the relationships among compilers, assemblers, interpreters, and machine instructions are given in Figure 5.2.

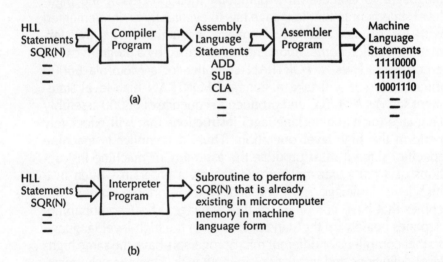

Figure 5.2 Compiler and Interpreter

When a computer system is composed of a large number of entities, such as multiple input/output terminals than can be used simultaneously, printers, disk drives, magnetic tapes, and communications interfaces, a program to manage and allocate these resources is essential. Programs of this type are called *operating systems.* Operating systems relieve the programmer of the necessity to know and understand the detailed electronic and mechanical operation of the peripheral devices. An operating system command can store a file created by the user on disk memory and allow him or her to retrieve the information by calling the file by name from a disk with another operating system command. An operating system can also manage the execution of programs by multiple users at the same time on a single computer. Although typically used with minicomputers and larger computers, operating systems are available for microcomputers. Two of the most popular operating systems for microcomputers are CP/M and Unix.™ (Unix is a trademark of the Western Electric Corporation.)

5.2. • SOFTWARE DESIGN METHODOLOGY

When computers began proliferating as viable commercial products in the 1950s, programming developed as an art and without the standard methodology that was available in the field of engineering, for example. With programming tasks aided by the introduction of the high-level language FORTRAN in 1956, software production increased, but the design of programs was random, intuitive, and not amenable to debugging.

5.2.1. • Structured Programming

A concept that is finding its way into practice and has influenced the development of some of the newer high-level languages is *structured programming.* Professor Nicholas Wirth has defined structured programming as "the formulation of programs as hierarchical, nested structures of statements and objects of computation."[1] As one would with any complex problem, the programmer decomposes the problem into a hierarchical structure for ease of understanding and management. The term *stepwise refinement* is often associated with structured programming. A common attribute of structured programming is the absence of GO TO statements. These statements perform unconditional branches in the program from one area to another that lead to difficulty in understanding, debugging, and modifying such programs. It is important to note that the absence of GO TO statements does not in itself produce a structured program.

From a management point of view, structured programming addresses the increasing life-cycle cost associated with software. It does this by encouraging the programmer to design software "top-down" from larger concepts to smaller, independent modules that can be implemented as manageable blocks of code. In this way, troubleshooting, maintenance, and modifying of the software are enhanced since a particular task performed by the program can be isolated to a specific module of code in the hierarchical structure.

An example using no particular language, but English-type statements, will illustrate a simple form of structure. The different modules of the program are labeled as procedures and are bounded by begin-end statement pairs.

```
procedure  calculate product cost

begin
        calculate labor cost L
        calculate materials cost M
        calculate overhead cost O
        total cost    T = L + M + O
end


procedure calculate unit selling price

begin
        calculate unit profit P
        unit selling price = T + P
end


procedure calculate yearly profit

begin
        calculate estimated # of units sold annually N
        yearly profit = N*P
end
```

In this sample program, there are three procedures. Each procedure, in turn, contains sub-elements of the main calculation. In this fashion, errors in the program can be isolated to specific procedures. The same concept is illustrated pictorially in the flowcharts in Figure 5.3, depicting the various sublevels in the decomposition of a hypothetical program A.

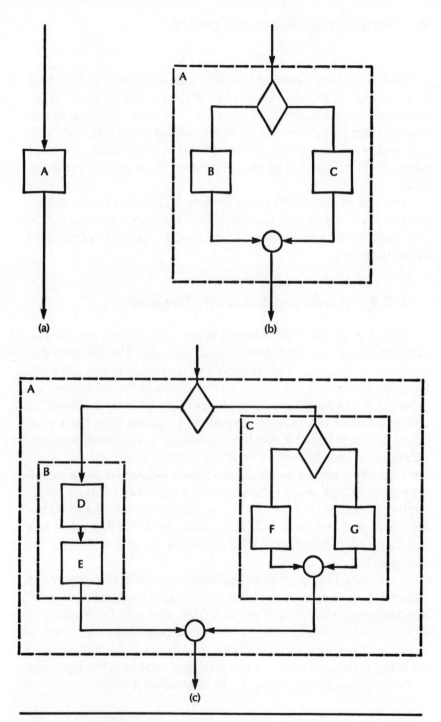

Figure 5.3 (a) Program A
         (b) Decomposition of Program A
         (c) Further Decomposition of Program A

Structured programming was advocated in 1965 by Professor E.W. Dijkstra of the University of Eindhoven, Netherlands.[2] Also, Bohm and Jacopini identified three basic structures that were sufficient to implement the logic of flowchartable programs.[3] The idea of stepwise refinement was promoted by Professor Wirth in a 1971 paper, further establishing the principles of structured programming.[4]

The use of structured programming will continue to expand, particularly since the popular high-level languages such as Pascal and Ada are inherently well-structured and conducive to structured software design.

5.2.2. • Hardware, Software, Firmware

The physical portions of the computer system such as the CPU, memory, and so on are the computer *hardware*. The program that is stored in memory and runs on the hardware is the *software*. Usually, the software can be modified easily in the computer. If a program is "burned" in read-only memory (ROM), it cannot be changed unless the ROM is physically removed from the circuit board and replaced by another containing a modified program. Programs of this type contained in ROM are termed *firmware*. Firmware is a means to amortize labor-intensive software development over high volume production of read-only memory chips. High density digital chips follow the familiar semiconductor learning curve that results in a 27% decrease in the selling price of a device for each doubling of the cumulative volume sold as shown in Figure 5.4.

By contrasting programming labor cost trends, as shown in Figure 5.5, it can be seen that it is very advantageous to develop standard programs, store them in ROMs, and sell the firmware in ROMs to take advantage of the semiconductor learning curve.

Assembly language instructions usually consist of an *operation code* (op code) and one or more *operands* related to the operation to be performed. For example, an instruction to move data from

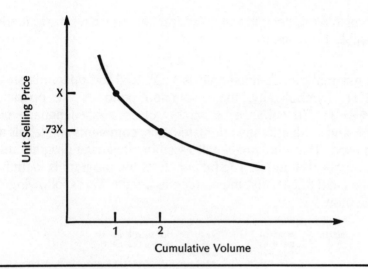

Figure 5.4 Semiconductor Learning Curve

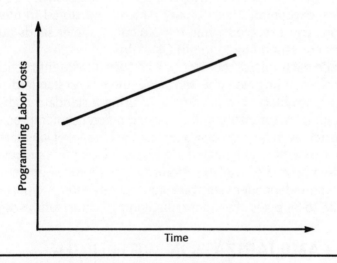

Figure 5.5 Increasing Programming Labor Costs

register 1 to register 2 in a microprocessor might have the following assembly language form:

MOV   r2, r1

The assembly level mnemonic is MOV and the operands are r2 and r1. Symbolically, the instruction performs the operation r2 ◄—— r1. To enhance readability of assembly language programs and to identify specific statements, comments and labels are also used. The following small assembly language program adds two numbers A and B. The beginning of the program is identified by the label BEGIN and the comments are the words following the semicolon.

```
BEGIN      READ A;        read in the value of A
           READ B;        read in the value of B
           ADD A, B;      add A and B
           JMP BEGIN;     go to BEGIN statement and start over
```

Recall that each of the four assembly language statements has a one-to-one correspondence with a pattern of 1's and 0's as machine language. The assembler program reads mnemonics, such as those given in the example add program, and produces binary code for machine execution. These binary patterns are stored in memory locations and executed when the program counter sends out the address corresponding to the BEGIN label.

Since each microprocessor has its own unique instruction set and corresponding assembly language, there is no standardization among assemblers. The advantage of using a standard high-level language is that transportability among different microprocessors can be achieved through compilers for the high-level language that produce assembly language code for the target microprocessor.

Assemblers are available from the microprocessor manufacturers and independent software houses. Assemblers typically require 2K to 8K bytes of memory, depending on the features offered.

5.3 • FAMILIARIZATION WITH HIGH-LEVEL LANGUAGES

The material presented in this section will briefly cover four popular high-level languages: BASIC, FORTRAN, Pascal, and Ada. BASIC and FORTRAN have been in use for relatively long periods of time while Pascal, and particularly Ada, are relatively new languages.

5.3.1 • BASIC

BASIC stands for the Beginner's All-purpose Symbolic Instruction Code that was developed at Dartmouth College and is probably the easiest of all languages to learn and use. Its statements are almost direct English and are written in free format (no special tabulation, spacing, and alignment required). In free format, extra blank spaces are ignored. A typical BASIC program will provide a flavor of the language. The numbers to the left of each statement are used for identification. BASIC statements are executed in ascending numerical order.

```
10      INPUT A, B, C, D
20      LET SUM = A+B+C+D
30      LET AVG = SUM/4
40      PRINT AVG
50      GO TO 10
60      END
```

As seen from reading the statements, this BASIC program calculates the average of the values in A, B, C, and D and prints the result. After printing, the program begins again and reads in new values of A, B, C, and D. Other BASIC example statements include:

```
READ         40  READ X, Y, Z
IF/THEN      50  IF SIN(x) = .5 THEN 80
GO TO        80  GO TO 95
```

There are also structured versions of BASIC that support some structured programming techniques. BASIC is usually interpreted and is being offered in ROM by many microprocessor manufacturers.

5.3.2 • FORTRAN

FORTRAN, which stands for Formula Translation, is one of the most widely used of all high-level languages. It is aimed primarily at scientific computing, but is utilized in many different types of applications. Conventional FORTRAN does not encourage structured programming. FORTRAN compilers exist for almost all minicomputers and most microprocessors.

The breadth of the FORTRAN language prohibits its detailed description in this context. However, some examples of its features will be presented for illustrative purposes. Before presenting the examples, the following definitions of words and symbols relative to FORTRAN are necessary:

```
DIMENSION  Names and declares the size of an array
INTEGER    Defines a variable as an integer
REAL       Defines a variable as a real number
+          Addition
-          Subtraction
*          Multiplication
/          Division
**         Exponentiation
GT.        Greater than
GE.        Greater than or equal to
LT.        Less than
LE.        Less than or equal to
EQ.        Equal to
NE.        Not equal to
```

Even though these definitions apply to FORTRAN, they are commonly used by other high-level languages.

An example FORTRAN program follows:

```
DIMENSION A(4), B(2)
INTEGER NUMBER
REAL VALUE
VALUE = 2.71**(10.)
NUMBER = 8
A(1) = 4.0
IF (A(1).LE.0.0) GO TO 30
A(2) = A(1) ** 3.5
- - - - - - - - - -
- - - - - - - - - -
- - - - - - - - - -
```

Like many high-level languages, FORTRAN provides a library of mathematical functions. These functions include:

```
ABS       Absolute value
ALOG      Natural log
ALOG10    Common log
SIN       Trigonometric sine
SQRT      Square root
```

In summary, FORTRAN compilers exist for numerous minicomputers and microprocessors. There has been a large software investment in FORTRAN over the last 25 years and because of this factor, FORTRAN is still widely used. However, FORTRAN in general does not lend itself to structured software design, and thus it will probabaly lose popularity to Pascal and Ada in new applications in the 1980's.

5.3.3 • Pascal

Pascal is a high-level programming language that was developed by Professor Nicolas Wirth of the Eidgenhossiche Technische Hochschule in Zurich, Switzerland.[5] The language was named after the seventeenth-century mathematician, Blaise Pascal, who invented one of the earliest calculators. Blaise Pascal was the son of a French tax collector and developed a mechanical adder utilizing interlocking cogs and wheels while he was still a teenager. This adding machine was known as the Pascaline. Because of the cheap cost of manual accounting labor and concerns about maintenance, the Pascaline was not a commercial success.

The language Pascal is important because it is one of the first to successfully embody in a uniform manner the concepts of structured programming. Because Pascal provides the framework for imparting structure to a program, it can enhance the approach to problem solving if properly applied.

Pascal has what is known as strong data typing in that it requires all variables that are used in the program to be declared "up front" as to type (real, integer, Boolean, character, etc.). The declarations can then be used to perform checks in the program to determine if the variables are being used improperly or are taking on values that exceed prespecified limits. These checks can be made during compilation of the code, and thus, errors can be detected before executing the program. Pascal programs, if written properly, can be easy to read and follow. As an example, let us look at a small Pascal program that finds the average of M numbers. The information enclosed by (* *) is treated as a comment by the Pascal compiler and is not executed as part of the program. Also, note that structuring of the program can be emphasized by levels of indentation to block off portions of the program.

```
(*PROGRAM TO CALCULATE AVERAGE OF M NUMBERS*)
PROGRAM   AVGCALC (INPUT,OUTPUT);
VAR  I,M : INTEGER
         AVG,NUMB,TOTAL : REAL
BEGIN
READ (M);
TOTAL :=0;
FOR  I : = 1 TO  M  DO
         BEGIN
         READ(NUMB);
         TOTAL : = TOTAL + NUMB
         END;
AVG : = TOTAL/M;,
WRITELN   ('AVERAGE IS =' , AVG)
END.
```

Even though the Pascal language has not been discussed, the general flow of the program can be followed. The underlined words are reserved words that are part of the Pascal language and understood by compiler to have a specific meaning and/or operation. Briefly looking at the program from the first line, the following operations are performed:

```
line 1           comment
line 2           naming Pascal program as AVGCALC
lines 3,4        declaring variables I and M to be integers
                 and AVG, NUMB, and TOTAL to be reals
line 5           BEGIN statement to block out portion of
                 program.  The last statement, END. in the
                 program pairs with this BEGIN.
line 6           reading in the number of numbers to be
                 used in average calculation
line 7           setting total = 0 initially
line 8           for M times, perform the operations
                 between the following BEGIN-END pair
line 9           BEGIN statement paired with END statement
                 on line 12
line 10          read in number to be used in average
                 calculation
line 11          add this number to total
line 12          END statement.  Keep performing operations
                 between BEGIN on line 9 and this END
                 until we have used M numbers.
line 13          calculate average
line 14          write out AVERAGE IS = _____
line 15          END statement that is paired with
                 BEGIN on line 5.  End of program.
```

As discussed in the FORTRAN section, Pascal also provides user library functions to perform squaring, square roots, and so on.

Pascal is widely supported by microcomputer manufacturers and is one of the languages of the 1980's. Its built-in structure is conducive to good programming style, and because of this, it will probably see its popularity increase in the 1980's.

5.3.4 • Ada

Ada is a high-order language sponsored by the U.S. Department of Defense (DoD) and is the culmination of requirements initiated in 1975.[6] The design of Ada took advantage of the lessons learned from predecessor languages as well as the latest thinking in structured design methodology. Ada was named after Ada Augusta, an Englishwoman who was the countess of Lovelace. Ada was a gifted mathematician who lived in the early 1800's and worked with Charles Babbage on the design of his "Analytical Engine." This device, which was never built by Babbage, would have been the first to embody the idea of a programmable computer that could be used for different types of calculations. Ada, who was also the daughter of Lord Byron, studied Babbage's design and published a series of notes entitled, "Observations on Mr. Babbage's Analytical Engine." Babbage proposed entering data into and controlling his Analytical Engine through the use of punched cards based on those invented by Frenchman Joseph Jacquard for controlling looms. Ada noted the similarity by stating that the "Analytical Engine weaves algebraic patterns." Ada died at the age of 36 and is credited by some as being the first computer programmer.

The requirements for Ada proceeded through a sequence called Strawman (1975), Woodenman (1975), Tinman (1976), Ironman (1978), and Steelman (1979). Universities, industry, and the three military services all commented on and provided input to the language specifications.

After a series of competitive awards, the language design proposed by CII-Honeywell-Bull of France was selected. This candidate language was known as the Green language throughout its development and renamed Ada on May 2, 1979. The Green language design team was based in Paris and was led by Jean Ichbiah.

Ada is meant to address a wide variety of applications. Ada was influenced by Pascal and thus offers some of the facilities of Pascal. In addition, Ada offers features found only in specialized languages. Ada emphasizes modularity, the ability to handle real-time applications, the development of concurrent programs, and reliability and maintainability.

As in Pascal, Ada requires the declaration of program variables and their type. Especially noteworthy is that Ada supports the separate compilation of program modules for ease of software development and debugging.

An example of a simple Ada program to find the average of three integers will serve to introduce the language. Comments in Ada are indicated by two dashes,– –. Underlined words indicate Ada key words. This averaging program is defined as a procedure that is a subprogram of an Ada program. This procedure could be compiled separately.

```
PROCEDURE AVG IS      - -   procedure name
      A, B, C :    INTEGER;  - -  declare three integer variables
      AVG   :    FLOAT;   - -  declare a floating point variable
BEGIN
      GET(A);     - -  read value and deposit in A
      GET(B);     - -  read value and deposit in B
      GET(C);     - -  read value and deposit in C
      AVG : = (A+B+C)/3.0;  - -    calculate average and deposit in AVG
      PUT(AVG);  - -  print out value of average
   END  AVG;     - -  terminate procedure
```

As in Pascal, BEGIN and END statements bound program segments. Ada (and also Pascal) permits the declaration of user-defined data types *into* types such as INTEGER, FLOAT, and so on.

The following procedures illustrate examples of these types. The first is called a data type and the second is an enumeration type. Note no spaces are permitted between characters in procedure names, and thus, an underscore must be used if separation for clarity is desired.

```
PROCEDURE      NEW_TYPE  IS          - -        procedure name
         TYPE RED IS NEW INTEGER;    - -        RED is a new type
         TYPE WHITE IS NEW INTEGER;  - -        WHITE is a new type
         TYPE BLUE IS NEW INTEGER;   - -        BLUE is a new type

         R:RED;                      - -        R is of type RED
         W:WHITE;                    - -        W is of type WHITE
         B:BLUE;                     - -        B is of type BLUE
         X:RED;
BEGIN
         W:=0;                       - -        W can be assigned
                                                an integer value
         Z:= R+X;                    - -        variables of same type can be
                                     - -        added
         B:= B+B                     - -        ditto
   END     NEW_TYPE


PROCEDURE ENUMERATION_TYPE IS        - -        procedure
   TYPE DAY IS
         (MON, TUES, WED, THURS, FRI);  - -     enumeration type
   TYPE D:DAY;                       - -        variable D is of type DAY
   TYPE I: INTEGER;                  - -        variable I is of type INTEGER
BEGIN
         IF D = MON THEN             - -        check to see if D is Monday
            I:= I+1;                 - -        if it is, add one to I
         END IF;                     - -        end if statement
END ENUMERATION_TYPE;                - -        end procedure
```

An innovation in Ada is the program unit called a *task*. A task provides the facilities for concurrent programming. Concurrent programming, in turn, offers the potential of increasing program execution speed by allowing some operations to be performed in parallel. Also, many real systems operate in a concurrent fashion (banks, airlines, etc.) and can utilize the task features for ease of implementation. Tasks have a specific declaration and are started by an INITIATE statement. The declaration includes a specification portion that defines the resources provided by the task and a body portion that contains the statements to be executed by the task. A task cannot normally be exited unless it has completed its execution. The following example of a task declaration and initiation for independent tasks will serve to illustrate these concepts.

```
PROCEDURE       START_UP IS                    - -    procedure
      TASK CHECK_FEEDSTOCK;                     - -    task declaration
      TASK BODY CHECK_FEEDSTOCK IS              - -    first task
      - - statements for checking feedstock    - -    task statements
      END CHECK_FEEDSTOCK;                      - -    end of first task
      TASK CHECK_POWER;                         - -    task declaration
      TASK BODY CHECK_POWER IS;                 - -    second task
         - - statements for checking power     - -    task statements
      END CHECK_POWER;                          - -    end of second task
      TASK CHECK_SAFETY;                        - -    task declaration
      TASK BODY CHECK SAFETY IS                 - -    third task
         - - statements for checking safety    - -    task statements
      END CHECK_SAFETY;                         - -    end
         -
         -
         -
BEGIN

      INITIATE CHECK_FEEDSTOCK, CHECK_POWER, CHECK SAFETY;

END START_UP;   - - exit after all tasks complete execution
```

For tasks that are not independent, task synchronization and communication must be implemented. Special statements and rules exist in Ada towards this end.

A number of architectures exist that support execution of Ada. For example, some software and hardware features of the Intel 432 32-bit microprocessor were influenced by Ada execution requirements.

Awareness of Ada is spreading in the industrial world as well as with military contractors. It promises to be one of the dominant languages of the 1980's and should be a factor in the software plans of all corporations that intend to be technologically competitive in this decade.

5.4 • CONSIDERATIONS IN SOFTWARE DEVELOPMENT, RELIABILITY, AND MAINTENANCE

Some insights into the "real" world of programming can be obtained by looking into the practical aspects of the development, reliability, and maintenance of the software after it has been delivered to the initial user. The major points that are presented concern the applicability of large-scale software development techniques to microcomputers, training and retraining of programmers, reliability, and software maintenance realities.

5.4.1 • Large Project Software Engineering Applied to Microcomputers

An interesting aspect of software development for microcomputers is the extent to which existing software engineering methods for large projects can be applied to small microcomputer projects. The term large projects, in this context, refers to the development of operating systems, compilers, and the like requiring numerous individuals to perform the tasks, as well as a high degree of coordination among these personnel. There have been extensive studies of large-scale software engineering problems and their conclusions; but in contrast, relatively few definitive guidelines have been established for small microcomputer project software development. The relationship between the two areas is worthy of examination.

In an experiment comparing large-scale software development to small project microcomputer software development, Barry W. Boehm tested the applicability of the following large project hypotheses:[7]

1. Large-project software engineering procedures can be cost-effectively tailored to small projects.
2. The choice of programming language is the dominant factor in small software product development.

3. Programming is the dominant activity in small software product development.
4. The "deadline effect" holds on small software projects and can be used to help manage software development.
5. Most of the code in a small application software product is devoted to "housekeeping."

The experiment consisted of evaluating two programming teams on a small-scale microcomputer software development project using different programming languages (Pascal and FORTRAN). The conclusions of the experiment were the following:

1. Hypothesis 1 was confirmed.
2. Hypothesis 2 was not confirmed. No significant difference was noted between the Pascal and FORTRAN teams.
3. Hypothesis 3 was not confirmed. Documentation and other activities consumed more time than programming.
4. Hypothesis 4 was confirmed. A small number of deadlines placed throughout the project can serve to accelerate development at the deadline intervals and thus help to meet the final completion deadline.
5. Hypothesis 5 was confirmed. The code required to perform the actual project functions was only a few percent of the total code. Larger percentages were devoted to data manipulation, error processing, and the like.

The bar chart of Figure 5.6 developed by Boehm[8] provides insight into the distribution of effort of the Pascal (P) and FORTRAN (F) teams on the microcomputer project (see next page).

5.4.2 • Training of Microcomputer Development Personnel

Another critical area in microcomputer system development is the training time required by the personnel involved. For example, assume computer hardware and software expertise are available in an independent, applied R & D organization or in a captive

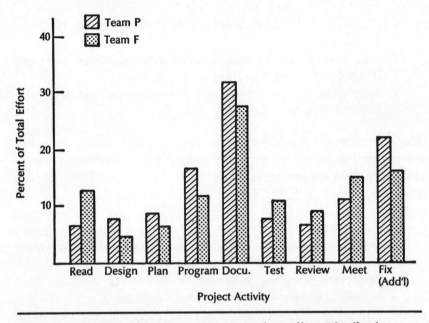

Figure 5.6 Small Scale Microcomputer Project Effort Distribution
(From B. Boehm, "An Experiment in Small-Scale
Applications Software Engineering," *IEEE Transactions of
Software Engineering,* Vol. SE-7, No. 5, Sept. 1981.)

group within a corporate organizational structure. Before mean-
ingful work can begin on a project, detailed information must be
obtained concerning the (1) Budget, (2) Application, (3) Schedule,
(4) Inventory, (5) Constraints, and (6) Specifications, or the BASICS,
of the system to be developed. The time involved in this initial
familiarization and learning effort is a critical and non-negligible
portion of the complete project development time. This time can
be used to advantage on other succeeding projects if some commonality can be established between projects. For example, the
commonality could be the use of the same type of microprocessor,
the same language, cross-assemblers on a common development
facility that have identical grammatical rules, and so on. Again,
this points out the importance of a well-planned and implemented
microcomputer hardware and software development facility to a
project's budget, quality, and time schedule.

5.4.3 • Software Reliability

The concept of software reliability is not as intuitive as is hardware reliability. Furthermore, techniques and theories of hardware reliability exist and are applied, whereas software reliability theories are not widely agreed upon or widely applied. For program sizes in the vicinity of 100 lines of code or more, it may take an extraordinary amount of time or, worse, be impossible to prove the correctness of the program code. Structured design can be of value in software reliability as well as in increasing productivity. "Information hiding" concepts in structured design discourage ripple effects in software changes and upgrades by maintaining defined interfaces among software modules. Required modifications can be made within a module without affecting its interface to the other portions of the program.

An important factor affecting software reliability is the specification given to the software implementors. In many cases, the specification can be incomplete or ambiguous, leading to incorrect program development relative to that desired. Alternately, the specification may be correct, but not totally implemented during software development. Specification languages that promote a computer-readable methodology for developing and checking specifications are extremely useful in reducing errors related to the specification. A number of these languages exist, used primarily by the military in large software development projects. A few such specification languages are also under development for industrial applications. Properly applied, these languages can significantly reduce costs in large computer-based, process control and manufacturing operations.

5.4.4 • Software Maintainability

Relative to hardware and software development, the area of software maintainability for microprocessors is not well understood or implemented. The significance of software maintenance is emphasized when numbers such as $80 per instruction are cited for software development costs as opposed to $4,000 per instruction for software maintenance costs.

With attention-grabbing numbers such as these, the logical question is, "What is meant by software maintenance?" Software maintenance takes place after delivery of the product to the initial user and encompasses not only corrections, but improvements or enhancements to the delivered computer system. It would be ideal if no maintenance were required on software after its delivery, but since undetected problems do occur during the early periods of product use, maintenance is inevitable. Furthermore, even if no such problems occur, there is usually a stage in the life of the computer system that requires adaptation to a modifed environment. Since software is usually more amenable to change than hardware, this adaptation is often accomplished by changing the program. In this case, the cause for concern is the effect the software changes will have on other, previously working portions of the hardware and software. The fact that these software maintenance changes will probably be accomplished in an operating or production situation and not in a highly supported development environment further adds to the possibility of creating new problems while correcting old ones. In many cases, the maintenance effort will be perpetuated by internal (to the software) and external (application environment) stimuli over the life of a software product, and it will not cease until the product is no longer used. An approximate percent distribution of the software maintenance tasks is presented in Figure 5.7.

In attempting to learn from the characteristics of software maintenance, some actions can be recommended. The first and most obvious is to assume that changes in the software and possibly the hardware of a computer system will be required after acceptance by the end user and to plan for these changes accordingly. This planning can take the form of using structured software development techniques to minimize interdependency among software modules. This methodology will result in a hierarchical approach to software system design and the use of a structured programming language for algorithm implementation. The planning for change should also apply to documentation supplied with the system.

The structure of the documentation should allow for the definition of modules and their interactions in such a way that changes or additions to these modules can be implemented without re-

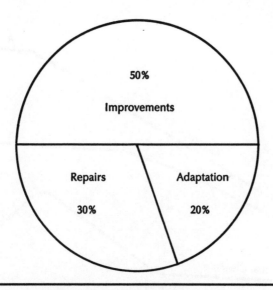

Figure 5.7 Approximate Percent Distribution of Software Maintenance Tasks

quiring modifications among related modules. Some insights to this approach are given by Daly.[9]

The maintenance of a software system, then, can be summarized by focusing on three of its characteristics as a function of time since its initial release. The first characteristic is the size of the software system. The size usually increases because of the number of enhancements and corrections added to the software, manifesting themselves in the form of new versions of the packages. This process continues until it becomes uneconomical in the form of effort required. At this stage, the software system tends to stabilize in terms of external changes. This behavior is illustrated by curve A in Figure 5.8 (see next page).

The second characteristic related to software maintenance is the complexity of the software system. The complexity is a direct result of the enhancements depicted in curve A and is caused by the software "blocks" added to the original version and the increasing interaction among them. Curve B in Figure 5.8 depicts this characteristic as a function of time.

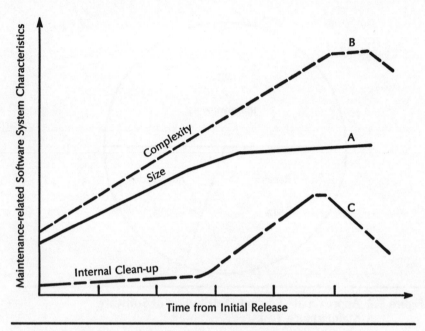

Figure 5.8 Summary of Maintenance-Related Software System Characteristics

The third manifestation of maintenance-related behavior of a system is the internal "clean-up" of code that has increased in size and complexity, as shown by curves A and B. As the system size levels off per curve A, attention turns to internal clean-up of the software. This internal clean-up, shown in curve C, is concerned with changes not usually visible to the user, but aimed at increasing the efficiency and reducing the size of the system.

Footnotes

1. N. Wirth, "On the Composition of Well-Structured Programs," *Computing Surveys*, Vol. 6, No. 4, Dec 1974, pp. 247–259.
2. E.W. Dijkstra, "Programming Considered as a Human Activity," *Proceedings of the IFIP Congress*, 1965, pp. 213–217.
3. C. Böhm and G. Jacopini, "Flow Diagrams, Turing Machines and Languages with Only Two Formulation Rules," *Communications of the ACM*, Vol. 9, No. 5, May 1966, pp. 366–371.

4. N. Wirth, "Program Development by Stepwise Refinement," *Communications of the ACM,* Vol. 14, No. 4, Apr 1971, pp. 221–227.

5. K. Jensen and N. Wirth, *Pascal User Manual and Report,* New York, New York, 1975.

6. *Reference Manual for the Ada Programming Language,* U.S. Department of Defense, 1980.

7. B. Boehm, "An Experiment in Small-Scale Applications Software Engineering," *IEEE Transactions of Software Engineering,* Vol. SE-7, No. 5, Sept. 1981, pp. 482–493.

8. B. Boehm, *op. cit.*

9. E. Daly, "Management of Software Development," *IEEE Transactions on Software Engineering,* Vol. SE-3, No. 3, May 1977, pp. 230–242.

ECONOMICS/ EVALUATION TECHNIQUES AND CRITERIA

Microprocessors are finding their way into more and more products, ranging from military weapons systems to consumer items. What are the reasons for this proliferation? Since consumer products are driven by the marketplace, cost must be a factor. But, are most products that incorporate microprocessors truly cost-effective or are microprocessors used so that the product can be touted as being "microprocessor-based?" In this chapter, we will examine some useful criteria for evaluating microprocessor applications and, where possible, specifically include economic considerations.

6.1 • MICROCOMPUTER SELECTION CRITERIA

In order to perform evaluations, we must have a basis of comparison. For microprocessors, bases of comparison include:

1. Instruction set
2. Architecture

3. Silicon-resident programs
4. Orientation of items 1 to 3 to support high-level language
5. Memory address space
6. Semiconductor technology
7. Operating environment
8. Support (including software, maintenance, and peripheral chips)
9. Second sourcing

In general, these items should be examined in light of the intended application of the microprocessor. For example, a microprocessor to be used in a hand-held electronic game should be evaluated based on different criteria from one that is to replace a minicomputer or small mainframe computer in performing complex numerical calculations on large amounts of data. The subset of instructions in the instruction set that has a high degree of applicability to the problem at hand will, naturally, be used more frequently by the programmer than irrelevant instructions. Thus, the speed of execution and memory storage requirements of the relevant instructions are important to consider for a specific application. As a means of microprocessor evaluation, instruction execution speed and corresponding storage requirements can be plotted for different applications with microprocessor type as a parameter. If hypothetical microprocessors M, I, Z, and R with different instruction sets are to be evaluated for input/output and arithmetic applications, a plot of program memory required versus instruction execution time for each application provides a comparison of the relative efficiencies of the processors. Figure 6.1 illustrates the form of these plots with hypothetical data.

Note that a redistribution of the microprocessors' positions occurs in the plots as a function of their application. The important conclusion to draw from this example is that the instructions in the instruction set that are relevant to the algorithm to be programmed should be used to evaluate a microprocessor's performance, and not the size of the instruction set as promoted in advertising. Another advantage of this method is that evaluation of the instruction set's applicability to a particular problem can be performed using

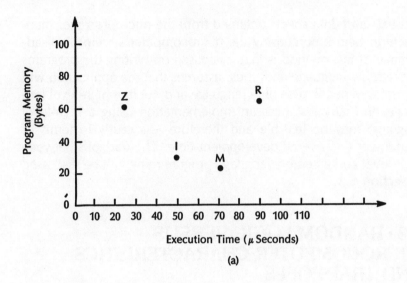

(a)

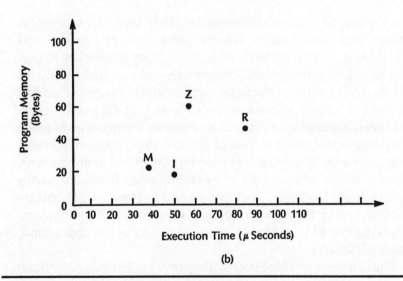

(b)

Figure 6.1 Memory versus Execution Time Plots for Different Microprocessors
(a) Input/Output Program
(b) Arithmetic Program

manuals and data sheets obtained from the microprocessor manufacturer before purchasing the microcomputer system. A disadvantage of this method is that it is based on writing the programs in assembly language and, thus, assumes that the application will be programmed in assembly language and not in a high-level language. In many instances an implementation using a high-level language may be feasible and therefore less costly in terms of manpower and overall development time. The tradeoffs between high-level and assembly language programming will be discussed in section 6.3.

6.2 · RANDOM LOGIC VERSUS MICROCOMPUTER CHARACTERISTICS AND TRADEOFFS

In the early days of microprocessors, they were introduced as random logic replacements. The microprocessor, as a general purpose device, can be customized by a program in memory to perform functions formerly implemented by random logic elements such as AND circuits, OR circuits, counters, shift registers, and so on. Since this application of microprocessors (as opposed to complex computational applications) is common, the question of when to use microprocessors in lieu of random logic frequently arises. There are two major issues that must be considered in this context. The first is the relative cost of microprocessor hardware versus random logic hardware, and the second is the cost of software development for the microprocessor-based system. If a microcomputer system cost is plotted against complexity of the application, Figure 6.2 results.

Now, if the additional cost of programming the microcomputer system is considered, the economic crossover point from random logic to microcomputer is moved upward on the complexity scale from A to B (see Figure 6.3).

Thus, the microcomputer software cost for random logic-type applications can seriously affect the tradeoff of microcomputer usage versus random logic. Another important factor is the number of units to be produced. If a large number of units is involved,

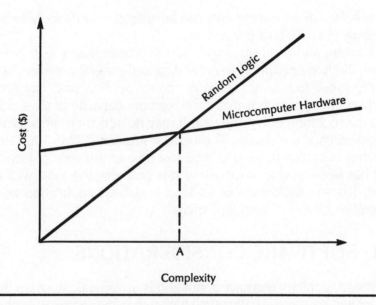

Figure 6.2 Microcomputer System Hardware Cost Versus Random Logic Cost

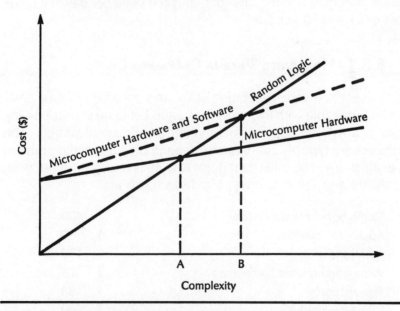

Figure 6.3 Microcomputer System Hardware and Software Cost Versus Random Logic Cost

the software development cost can be spread over these systems, resulting in a low cost per system.

Four-bit and eight-bit single chip microcomputers with a relatively limited amount of internal data and program memory are ideally suited for many logic and control applications. The only catch to this approach is that if the memory capacity of the single chip microcomputer is exceeded, it may be difficult or impossible to add additional memory. The Texas Instruments' TMS 1000 single-chip microcomputer is a good example of this type of device and has been around since 1974. It is probably the most widely used, lowest cost device of its kind and finds application as a controller for games and appliances.

6.3 • SOFTWARE CONSIDERATIONS

Considering microcomputer applications in general, software development costs are usually much higher than microprocessor chip costs. For example, software generation rates are typically estimated at from two to ten lines of debugged code per day at a labor cost of $1 to $10 per line!

6.3.1 • Hardware Versus Software Costs

Present software generation rates and associated labor costs are incompatible with the microcomputer. Let us take the following case of a hypothetical microcomputer development project. The numbers are typical, but naturally depend on the specific problem specifications. The important point to note is the contrast between hardware and software costs. Hardware costs are:

Single board microcomputer	$ 400
Additional memory	$ 300
Additional I/O	$ 150
Wiring and related hardware	$ 75
Power supply	$ 80
Labor (assembly)	$ 2000
TOTAL	$ 3305

Software costs are estimated as:

10K lines of code at a $5 per line (labor) = $50,000.

Software costs are much larger than microprocessor costs. The contrast points to the major problem in microcomputer development today—high software costs (labor-intensive) versus low hardware costs (high-volume production).

If software costs are to be compatible with microcomputer system hardware costs as given in the previous example, they should be approximately $3300. Thus, for 10,000 lines of code, the desired cost per line can be calculated as:

cost per line = $3300/10,000 lines = $.33

At the present time, the only two options available to achieve this goal are the use of high-level languages or standard firmware in ROMs that can be sold in high volume.

The divergent trends in labor versus microprocessor costs can be further analyzed by comparing the learning curve of semiconductor devices to software labor cost increases as a function of time. The cost of microprocessor hardware (COH) is assumed to follow the learning curve equation, Ke^{-2t} where K is the initial chip cost, t is years, and 2t assumes a doubling of volume in six month time periods. The cost of software labor (COL) is assumed to be linear, following the equation mt + b where m is the increase in labor cost/year, t is time in years, and b is the initial software cost.

In order to obtain an idea of the divergence in hardware and software costs, let us assign the following values.

K = initial cost of chip right after development = $ 250
m = labor cost increase per year = $ 7500
b = initial software development cost = $ 5 $\times 10^4$

Now, we can write:

$$COL = mt + b = 7500t + 5 \times 10^4$$
$$COH = Ke^{-2t} = 250e^{-2t}$$

The COL and COH curves using the assumptions stated are plotted in Figures 6.4 and 6.5, respectively.

6.3.2 · High-Level Language Versus Assembly Language

It is obvious that writing programs in a high-level language such as Pascal or Ada can result in high productivity and easier maintenance than writing the programs in assembly language. For example, it is easier for a programmer to write the expression

$$A: = \quad (SQRT(9.18))/(sin(6.28) * 896.312)$$

in a high-level language than to put together a series of relatively primitive assembly language instructions to perform the indicated operations. Also, a program written in a "standard" high-level language is portable since it can be run on any computer with a compiler for the language. The penalties for using a high-level language are threefold and are a result of the inefficiency of the compiler in generating assembly language code relative to a good assembly language programmer. The first penalty is in the amount of memory required. Since a high-level language compiler may generate more than twice the number of assembly language instructions to implement a particular set of operations than a good programmer, the amount of memory needed is increased. Second, the larger number of instructions generated by the compiler take longer to execute; therefore, they may be too slow for use in many real-time data acquisition and control systems. Third, the high-level language compiler program requires a large block of memory itself, and thus, the total memory required for the development of the software is increased.

Looking at the pros and cons of high-level language use, the trend will be to increase the use of high-level languages in microcomputer software development. Structured languages such as Pascal and Ada will increase programmer productivity and enhance associated documentation. Since memory costs are continuing to decrease, the additional memory costs necessitated by the use of a high-level language compiler will be more than offset by the decreased software labor cost. Assembly language will still be

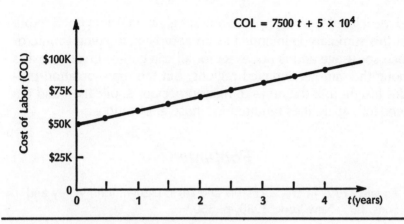

Figure 6.4 Cost of Software Labor versus Time

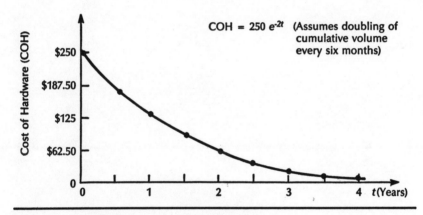

Figure 6.5 Semiconductor Learning Curve

required in high-speed, real-time applications where instruction execution times are critical and unnecessary delays cannot be tolerated. Also, some very high-volume, microprocessor-based products may be able to save significant memory costs by optimizing and compressing the programs by means of assembly language. Detailed analysis of this topic is given in Krutz, *Microprocessor and Logic Design*.[1]

As an aid to the reader, a summary of microprocessor word size, memory capacity requirements, instruction execution speed, and associated typical applications are given in Appendix B. Note that this summary is intended as an approximate guide to microprocessor usage and is not exact for all categories. Overlap exists among the various depicted regions, but the representation provides insight into the areas of microprocessor application and the attendant capabilities required for those applications.

Footnote

1. Ronald Krutz, *Microprocessors and Logic Design.* John Wiley and Sons, Inc., New York, 1980, p. 350.

Graphic or Control	ASCII (Hexa-decimal)	Graphic or Control	ASCII (Hexa-decimal)	Graphic or Control	ASCII (Hexa-decimal)
NULL	00	ACK	7C	1	31
SOM	01	Alt. Mode	7D	2	32
EOA	02	Rubout	7F	3	33
EOM	03	!	21	4	34
EOT	04	"	22	5	35
WRU	05	#	23	6	36
RU	06	$	24	7	37
BELL	07	%	25	8	38
FE	08	&	26	9	39
H. Tab	09	'	27	A	41
Line Feed	0A	(	28	B	42
V. Tab	0B	)	29	C	43
Form	0C	*	2A	D	44
Return	0D	+	2B	E	45
SO	0E	,	2C	F	46
SI	0F	-	2D	G	47
DCO	10	.	2E	H	48
X-On	11	/	2F	I	49
Tape Aux. On	12	:	3A	J	4A
X-Off	13	;	3B	K	4B

Appendix A: ASCII Character Set (continued next page)

Graphic or Control	ASCII (Hexa-decimal)	Graphic or Control	ASCII (Hexa-Decimal)	Graphic or Control	ASCII (Hexa-decimal)
Tape Aux. Off	14	<	3C	L	4C
Error	15	=	3D	M	4D
Sync	16	>	3F	N	4E
LEM	17	~	3F	O	4F
S0	18	[	5B	P	50
S1	19	/	5C	Q	51
S2	1A	]	5D	R	52
S3	1B	←	5E	S	53
S4	1C	↓	5F	T	54
S5	1D	@	40	U	55
S6	1E	blank	20	V	56
S7	1F	0	30	W	57
				X	58
				Y	59
				Z	5A

Appendix A (continued)

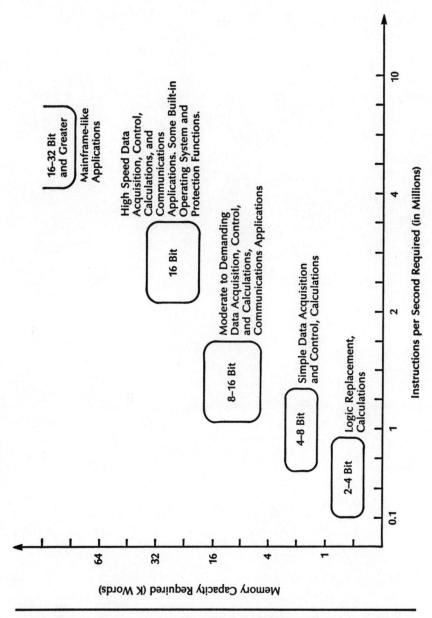

Appendix B: Microprocessor Applications and Required Capabilities

Glossary

Access Time—the interval from the time a stable memory address is presented to the memory to the time valid information is available at the memory outputs.

Accumulator—the internal microprocessor register(s) where data are stored and manipulated. Sometimes accumulators are used to transfer data into or out of the processor.

ACIA—abbreviation for Asynchronous Communications Interface Adapter. This chip is used for serial communications to and from the microprocessor.

Acoustic Coupler—a hardware device which is used to connect a computer system to the handset of a conventional telephone.

A/D—abbreviation for analog to digital.

Adder—a digital circuit that performs addition.

Address—the coded numerical value that is used to identify specific locations in memory.

Algorithm—a step-by-step procedure that leads to a problem solution.

Alphanumeric—refers to both letters and numbers.

ALU—abbreviation for Arithmetic Logic Unit. A principal component of a processor. An ALU performs arithmetic and logical operations, usually in binary form.

Analog—refers to a continuous range of values, usually current or voltage.

ANSI—abbreviation for American National Standards Institute. An organization that establishes standards, including some that relate to the computer industry.

ASCII—abbreviation for American Standard Code for Information Interchange. This refers to a code for representing alphanumeric characters and other symbols.

Assembler—a program that converts, on a one-to-one basis, symbolic names for processor instructions and variables to a form understandable by the processor. The symbolic names are referred to as assembly language.

Auxiliary Storage—usually refers to data or program storage other than main semiconductor or magnetic core memory, such as magnetic tape or disk.

Asynchronous—data transmission or event occurrences that are not regular or synchronized with a master clock.

Backplane—computer hardware that provides wiring and connectors for printed circuit cards.

BASIC—abbreviation for Beginner's All-purpose Symbolic Instruction Code. This is a popular computer language that uses English-like instructions, and is used primarily by non-professional programmers.

Baud—refers to a rate of data transmission. Formally, it is the reciprocal of the shortest pulse width in a data transmission sequence. It is usually interpreted as bits per second.

BCD—abbreviation for Binary Coded Decimal, a four-bit code used to represent the numbers 0 through 9.

Benchmark—a program used to evaluate the performance of a computer for a given application.

Bipolar—usually refers to semiconductor fabrication technology that involves two types of current carriers. Some examples are npn or pnp transistors.

Bit—binary digit.

Bit-slice—a "slice" of a processor in component form that can be used as a basic building block to build a processor of desired bit length. Bit slices are usually two or four bits wide and are bipolar technology.

Bootstrap—a small program to initialize a computer for operation.

Bug—an error or malfunction in hardware or software.

Byte—a grouping of 8 bits taken as a unit.

CAD—abbreviation for Computer-Aided Design.

Carry—a bit in the processor that indicates an arithmetic overflow or overflow of a shift register.

CCD—a Charge-Coupled Device memory. This is a serial memory of semiconductor nature.

Chip—a monolithic integrated circuit.

Clock—a master timing waveform for a computer system.

Coaxial Cable—a transmission line with the center conductor surrounded by a dielectric that is, in turn, surrounded by a conductor that serves as a shield. Coaxial cable has a determinable characteristic impedance.

Complement—the logical inverse of a bit or logic state. The complement of a logic 1 is a logic 0 and vice versa.

Compiler—a program that converts high-level, English-like programming language statements into assembly or machine language instructions. Conversion is usually a one-to-many operation.

CPU—abbreviation for Central Processing Unit or central processor.

CRT—abbreviation for Cathode-Ray Tube. Usually refers to a video terminal.

Cycle Time—the time required to access memory and then have the ability to access memory again.

D/A—abbreviation for digital to analog.

Data base—a collection of data files organized for ease of access.

Diskette—a flexible plastic disk used as the storage medium in a floppy disk drive.

DMA—abbreviation for Direct Memory Access. The act of transferring data directly to and from memory without going through the processor.

Duplex—bidirectional data communications capability.

Dynamic—refers to random access memories that store data as charges on capacitors that must be regularly "refreshed" to retain the stored information.

Editor—a program that permits a user to enter data into a computer file and then retrieve, modify, and transmit the information.

EEPROM—abbreviation for Electrically Erasable Programmable Read Only Memory. A reusable, MOS Read Only Memory chip that provides for in-circuit, electrical modification of its contents while maintaining nonvolatility.

EPROM—abbreviation for Erasable Programmable Read Only Memory. A MOS Read Only Memory whose total contents are erasable by illumination of the chip with ultraviolet light, usually through a quartz window in the package. This erasure is done out of circuit. The contents of the EPROM are nonvolatile.

Fetch—to retrieve instructions or data from computer memory.

File—a collection of data records which are treated as a unit.

Firmware—programs stored in Read Only Memory.

Flag—a status signal or pattern that can be generated in either hardware or software. It can be examined to determine subsequent actions.

Flip-flop—a two-state circuit that acts as a one-bit memory.

FORTH—a computer language, used particularly on microcomputers.

FORTRAN—a high-level computer language oriented toward scientific applications.

FSK—abbreviation for Frequency Shift Keying, a technique of encoding data for transmission using signals of different frequency.

Full Duplex—the ability of a transmission line to transmit information in both directions simultaneously.

Glitch—an unwanted pulse or series of pulses that usually result in improper operation of a digital circuit.

Ground—a potential used as a reference for all other voltages in a circuit. Ground potential is usually zero volts.

Ground loop—a current path through earth ground that generates undesirable potential differences in a circuit's ground path.

Half-duplex—a bidirectional communications link which can be used in only one direction at a time.

Hamming Code—an error detecting and correcting code that is implemented by adding additional bits to the data word to be transmitted.

Handshake—a part of a data transfer mechanism that involves the exchange of control signals such as data ready, data received, and so on to accomplish transmission or reception of information.

Hard-sectored—dividing a magnetic disk into sectors by physical means such as holes.

Hard-wired—the implementation of a function by circuits and wiring instead of by programming.

Hexadecimal—base 16 number representation.

High-Level Language—computer programming language that uses English-like statements to perform relatively complex operations. Each high-level statement is usually converted into many of the simpler, machine instructions that are native to the computer. FORTRAN, Pascal, and BASIC are examples of high-level languages.

IEEE-488—a parallel interface standard for an 8-bit data path.

I²L—integrated injection logic. A bipolar integrated circuit logic family.

Input/Output—that portion of a microcomputer performing transfer of data (I/O).

Instruction Cycle—the sequence of fetching an instruction from program memory and executing it.

Interface—the boundary between functional modules and the means of exchanging information between the modules.

Interpreter—a program that reads each high-level language statement and performs the operation indicated by executing a predefined sequence of machine language instructions.

Interrupt—the act of causing the temporary suspension of an executing program in a computer and transferring execution to another interrupt program. The interrupt program usually is a high priority program that performs data transfer or emergency-handling activities.

Karnaugh Map—a pseudo-graphical means for minimizing Boolean functions used in logic design.

Latency—the time delay between the request for data and the initiation of the data transfer.

LCD—abbreviation for Liquid Crystal Display.

LED—abbreviation for Light-Emitting Diode.

Linking Loader—a program that completes assembler-originated address calculations.

LSB—abbreviation for Least Significant Bit.

LSI—abbreviation for Large Scale Integration, referring to a level of integrated circuit fabrication density used for microprocessors and large semiconductor memories.

Machine Language—the instructions specific to a particular computer and represented in binary form.

Macro—a group of instructions that an assembler recognizes by a name and is invoked every time the name is called.

Macro Assembler—an assembler which is capable of implementing macro instructions.

Magnetic bubble memory—a semiconductor-based memory technique using magnetic domains to achieve nonvolatile data storage.

Mark—a term meaning a logic 1.

Memory—the portion of a computer which is used to store programs and data.

Memory-mapped I/O—a scheme in which the addresses of the input/output portions of the microcomputer appear as memory locations, thus allowing any instructions referencing memory to also be used as I/O instructions.

Microcomputer—a computer consisting of a microprocessor, memory, input/output means, and timing references.

Microcontroller—a microcomputer which is aimed at control applications.

Microprocessor—a central processing unit (CPU) that includes an arithmetic logic unit (ALU) and control circuits residing on one or more integrated circuit chips.

Microprogramming—a technique that utilizes programs in a memory called a microstore to implement instruction decoding and control functions in a processor.

Mnemonic—a name given as a memory aid to identify a computer assembly or machine language instruction.

Modem—a modulator, demodulator for transmitting and receiving digital signals over a telephone line.

Monitor—a program that provides basic program loading and execution commands for user interaction with a computer.

MOS—abbreviation for Metal-Oxide-Semiconductor fabrication technology for integrated circuits.

MSI—abbreviation for Medium Scale Integration level of density for integrated circuit fabrication. Typical MSI circuits are counters, shift registers, and so on.

MSB—abbreviation for Most Significant Bit.

NMOS—abbreviation for n-channel MOS semiconductor fabrication technology.

Noise—unwanted electrical signals introduced into a circuit, usually by inductive or capacitive coupling.

Object code—binary representation of an instruction that can be directly executed by a computer.

Octal—a number representation system using base 8.

Op code—an operation code portion of a computer instruction that, when decoded, indicates the action(s) to be performed to implement the instruction.

Operating Systems—a program that manages the resources of a computer system for the user.

Pascal—a high-level programming language with constructs that encourage structured programming.

Peripheral—a device connected to a computer, usually as a receiver or transmitter of data.

PIA—abbreviation for Peripheral Interface Adapter, a chip used to implement I/O functions in a microcomputer.

PLA—abbreviation for Programmed Logic Array. Integrated circuits used for read only memory applications and implementation of logic functions.

PL/M—a high-level programming language for microcomputers.

PMOS—abbreviation for p-channel MOS semiconductor fabrication technology.

PPI—abbreviation for Programmable Peripheral Interface. A chip used to implement I/O functions in a microcomputer.

PROM—abbreviation for Programmable Read Only Memory.

Propagation delay—the time it takes for a signal to pass through a logic element or wire.

Radix—the base of a number system.

RAM—abbreviation for Random Access Memory.

Refresh—the act of restoring charge on a capacitive storage element in a MOS dynamic memory.

Register—a small capacity memory, usually located in the processor.

Resident Assembler—an assembler residing on the processor for which it generates machine instructions.

Rise time—the time it takes for a logic signal to go from its low to high state.

ROM—abbreviation for Read Only Memory.

Schottky bipolar—bipolar semiconductor fabrication technology known for its enhanced switching speed over conventional bipolar technology.

SDLC—abbreviation for Synchronous Data Link Control. A computer communications protocol introduced by IBM.

Simplex—data transmission in one direction only.

Simulator—a program that "acts" as if it is another computer. It is used for software development and testing.

Soft sector—the region of a disk that is defined by additional information stored on the disk itself.

Source program—the user readable form of a program in contrast to a binary form executable by a computer.

Speed power product—a figure of merit for fabrication technology that is the product of propagation delay through a transistor or gate and the corresponding power consumed by that transistor or gate.

SSI—abbreviation for Small Scale Integration, referring to a level of integrated circuit fabrication density used for gates and flip-flops.

Static memory—a random access memory that does not require refreshing.

Synchronous—associated with a master clock or periodic timing source.

Technology—a fabrication method and materials used to implement integrated circuits.

Track—a "ring" on a disk that serves as storage for digital data.

Transmission Line—the physical means of transmitting analog and digital waveforms that exhibit certain characteristics as a function of length, construction, and type of information transmitted.

Tri-state—a logic element that has three possible output states—logic 1, logic 0, and high impedance (open circuit).

TTL—abbreviation for Transistor-Transistor Logic. A bipolar digital logic family.

Twisted pair—a pair of wires twisted together and used for data transmission.

UART—abbreviation for Universal Asynchronous Receiver/Transmitter which is used for asynchronous serial data transmission and reception.

USART—abbreviation for Universal Synchronous/Asynchronous Receiver/Transmitter, which is used for synchronous and asynchronous data transmission and reception.

UV source—an ultraviolet light source used to erase reusable, programmable, read only memories (EPROMs).

Vectored Interrupt—an interrupt to a computer program execution that causes control to transfer to the corresponding interrupt service program without having to determine which of several possible sources initiated the interrupt.

Virtual memory—a memory addressing system that controls the different types of memories in a computer system so that the programmer is given the impression that he or she has a large amount of random access memory available.

VLSI—abbreviation for Very Large Scale Integration, referring to a level of integrated circuit fabrication density used for complex computer systems on a chip.

Word—a collection of bits treated as a group.

Writable Control Store (WCS)—a read/write memory which is used as the storage for microprograms that implement a processor's control mechanisms.

Index

access time, 48
accumulator, 40
active low, 36
Ada, 14, 69, 85, 97–99
ALGOL, 7
ALU, 1, 29, 63
architecture, 63
arithmetic processing chip, 79
ASCII, 74, 119, 120
assembler, 84, 86
assembly language, 17, 84, 86, 116

Babbage, Charles, 3, 14, 97
Backus, John, 7
Bardeen, John, 10
BASIC, 84, 86, 93
Bell Laboratories, 3, 10, 53
Bendix G–10, 8
Binac, 5
binary
   numbers, 23
   states, 22
bipolar, 11, 43, 44
Bletchley Park, 5
Böhm, C., 90
Brattain, Walter, 10
bubble memory, 55, 56
buffer, 40
Burroughs, 8, 10
bus, 2
   address, 2
   control, 2
   data, 2

Cambridge University, 5
CCD, 54

CMOS, 46, 47
COBOL, 7
Colossus, 5
Columbia University, 3
compilier, 17, 85, 86
Computer Control Company, 9
Control Data, 7, 8, 10
cost, programming, 17
counter, 35–38
CP/M, 87
Cray, Seymour, 7
cross assembler, 84

DEC
   PDP–1, 8
   PDP–5, 8
   PDP–8, 8
   PDP–11, 13, 14
   VAX, 14
decoder, 29
demultiplexer, 31
development system, 75–77
Digital Equipment Corporation, 8
Dijkstra, E.W., 90
disk, 58–60
   flexible, 58
   floppy, 58
   Winchester, 58
distributed processing, 18, 19
DMA, 75
DOS, 9

EAROM, 49
Eckert, J. Presper, 4
Edvac, 4
EEPROM, 49

EEROM, 49
Eindhoven, 90
Eniac, 4
EPROM, 48

Faggin, Federico, 12
Fairchild Semiconductor, 11
Field Effect Transistor (FET), 11
firmware, 90
fixed point, 41
flip-flop, 33
floating point, 41
Forrester, Jay W., 5
FORTRAN, 7, 85, 87, 93–95
full adder, 27, 29

GE, 7
glossary, 123–132
GPIB, 80

hardware, 90
hexadecimal, 24
High-Level Language (HLL), 85, 116
High-Order Language (HOL), 85
HMOS, 46
Hoff, Marrcian E., 11
Honeywell, 7, 9
hybrid circuitry, 10

IBM, 3, 6, 7, 9, 53
IEEE–488, 80, 81
Intel, 11, 56, 69, 70
    432, 13, 14
    4004, 11, 12
    8008, 12
    8022, 13
    8048, 13
    8080, 12
interface, 78
interpreter, 85, 86
interrupt, 40

Jacopini, G., 90

Kilburn, Tom, 5
Kilby, Jack, 11
Krutz, Ronald, 117

Librascope LGP–30, 8

machine language, 17, 83, 86
Manchester University, 5
Mauchley, John W., 4
memory, 47–61
    cost per bit, 61
microcoding, 67
microcomputer, 2
    selection criteria for, 109–112
microprocessor, 2
    applications, 121
    architecture, 63, 64
    building blocks, 38–42
    432, 69, 70
    6502, 65–68
    6800, 12, 13
    Z8000, 70, 71
    9900, 13
    68000, 13, 71–74
M.I.T., 3, 5
MNOS, 49
MOSFET, 11, 44
Motorola, 12
    6800, 12, 13
    68000, 13, 71–74
multiplexer, 31
multiprogramming, 10

National Semiconductor, 56
    GPCP, 12
    PACE, 13
NMOS, 44
nonvolatility, 47
NOVRAM, 51
Noyce, Robert, 11

Olsen, Kenneth, 8
operand, 90
operating system, 19, 86, 87

operation code, 90
OS/360, 10

Pascal, 85, 95, 96
PDP–1, 8
PDP–5, 8
PDP–8, 8
PDP–11, 8
PMOS, 44
processor, 1
program counter (PC), 41
program decomposition, 88, 89
programmer's workbench, 76–78

RAM, 50
  dynamic, 51
  static, 51
random logic, 112–114
RCA, 7, 11
refresh, 50
register, 34
  shift, 35
Remington Rand, 6
Rockwell, 56
  PPS–4, 12
ROM, 47
RS–232, 80
RS–422, 80
RS–423, 80

Schottky, 44
SDLC, 79, 80
semiconductor learning curve, 15,
    16, 91, 117
sequential logic, 32
Shannon, Claude E., 3
Shima, Masatoshi, 13
Shockley, William, 10

software, 90
  costs, 17, 115
  engineering, 100
  maintainability, 103–106
  reliability, 103
  training, 101
Sperry Rand, 10
stack pointer, 40
stepwise refinement, 87
Stibitz, George R., 3
structured programming, 87

table of combinations, 27
Texas Instruments, 56
  TMS 1000, 15
  9900, 13
transistor, 10
tri-state, 52
two's complement, 25, 26

UART, 74
Univac, 6
University of Pennsylvania, 5
Unix, 87
USART, 75
UV, 49

Varian Data Machines, 9
virtual memory, 10

Watson, Thomas J., 3
Whirlwind, 5
Wilkes, Maurice, 5
Williams, Frederick C., 5
Williams tube, 5
Wirth, Nicholas, 87, 90, 95

Zilog, 13
  Z80, 13
  Z8000, 13, 70, 71